ANSWERS
TO THE MOST
IMPORTANT
QUESTIONS
ABOUT THE
END TIMES

Books by Dr. John Hart

50 Things You Need to Know About Heaven
*Evidence for the Rapture: A Biblical Case for Pretribulationism**
Answers to the Most Important Questions About the End Times

*Editor and contributor

ANSWERS
TO THE MOST
IMPORTANT
QUESTIONS
ABOUT THE
END TIMES

DR. JOHN HART

BETHANYHOUSE
a division of Baker Publishing Group
Minneapolis, Minnesota

© 2016 by John F. Hart

Published by Bethany House Publishers
11400 Hampshire Avenue South
Bloomington, Minnesota 55438
www.bethanyhouse.com

Bethany House Publishers is a division of
Baker Publishing Group, Grand Rapids, Michigan

ISBN 978-0-7642-1785-2

Printed in the United States of America

Library of Congress Control Number: 2016931164

Note: Italics in Scripture added by the author for emphasis.

All Scripture quotations, unless otherwise indicated, are from the Holy Bible, *New Living Translation*, copyright © 1996, 2004, 2007 by Tyndale House Foundation. Used by permission of Tyndale House Publishers, Inc., Carol Stream, Illinois 60188. All rights reserved.

Scripture quotations identified AMP-CE are from the Amplified® Bible, copyright © 1954, 1958, 1962, 1964, 1965, 1987 by The Lockman Foundation. Used by permission. (www.Lockman.org)

Scripture quotations identified CEV are from the Contemporary English Version, copyright © 1991, 1992, 1995 by American Bible Society. Used by permission.

Scripture quotations identified ESV are from *The Holy Bible, English Standard Version*, copyright © 2000, 2001 by Crossway Bibles, a division of Good News Publishers. Used by permission. All rights reserved.

Scripture quotations identified HCSB are taken from the Holman Christian Standard Bible, copyright © 1999, 2000, 2002, 2003, 2009 by Holman Bible Publishers. Used by permission. Holman Christian Standard Bible, Holman CSB, and HCSB are federally registered trademarks of Holman Bible Publishers.

Scripture quotations identifies NASB are from the New America Standard Bible, copyright © 1960, 1962, 1963, 1968, 1971, 1972, 1973, 1975, 1977, 1995 by The Lockman Foundation. Used by permission. www.Lockman.org

Scripture quotations identified NIV are from the Holy Bible, New International Version®. NIV®. Copyright © 1973, 1978, 1984, 2011 by Biblica, Inc.™ Used by permission of Zondervan. All rights reserved worldwide. www.zondervan.com

Scripture quotations identified KJV are from the King James Version.

Scripture quotations identified NKJV are from the New King James Version, copyright © 1982 by Thomas Nelson, Inc. Used by permission.

Scripture quotations identified NET are from the NET Bible [New English Translation], copyright © 1996–2006 by Biblical Studies Press, L.L.C. http://netbible.com. Used by permission.

Scripture quotations identified GNT are from the Good News Translation, Second Edition. Copyright © 1992 by American Bible Society. Used by permission.

Scripture quotations identified CEB are from the Contemporary English Version © 1991, 1992, 1995 by American Bible Society. Used by permission.

Scripture quotations identified NRSV are from the New Revised Standard Version of the Bible, copyright © 1989, by the Division of Christian Education of the National Council of the Churches of Christ in the United States of America. Used by permission. All rights reserved.

Scripture quotations identified NJB are from THE NEW JERUSALEM BIBLE, copyright © 1985 by Darton, Longman & Todd, Ltd. and Doubleday, a division of Random House, Inc. Reprinted by permission.

Cover design by LOOK Design Studio

16 17 18 19 20 21 22   7 6 5 4 3 2 1

I wish to thank the Lord Jesus for helping me write and finally finish this book through some hard times. May it glorify him.

I also wish to thank my wonderful wife, Cindy, for her patience and encouragement through the writing process, and for her diligent proofreading of the manuscript.

Contents

Acknowledgments   9

1. Why Should I Be Interested in Bible Prophecy?   11

2. Are There Signs That We Are in the End Times?   21

3. What Is the Tribulation?   35

4. Will Christians Be Raptured and Escape the
   Tribulation?   51

5. How Can We Understand the Book of Revelation?   63

6. Who Is the Antichrist?   79

7. What Is the Role of Israel in the End Times?   91

8. What Nations Will Be in Power in the End Times?   107

9. What Is Armageddon?   123

10. What Is the Second Coming of Christ to the Earth?   145

11. What Is the Millennium?   159

12. What Is the Final Judgment, and the New Heaven and New
    Earth?   171

Acknowledgments

I am so grateful for the editorial staff, and especially for Andy McGuire. They were responsible for suggesting I write this book. I also want to thank Andy for his patience with me in the writing process, offering support and encouragement in numerous ways. I appreciate everyone at Bethany House who has helped in making this book possible.

1

Why Should I Be Interested in Bible Prophecy?

On January 22, 2015, the Doomsday Clock was set at three minutes to midnight. Midnight is the symbolic time on the clock when such global disasters take place that the continued existence of humanity will be threatened. The time on the clock can move closer to midnight as a result of unchecked climate change, the modernization of global nuclear weapons, and the increased number of massive nuclear weapons arsenals. The decision to increase or reduce the time left for human survival is made by a board of scientists and nuclear experts. The January 22, 2015, update is the closest the clock has been to Doomsday since 1984, when a climax of political and military tension was reached between the United States and the former Soviet Union.

It's no wonder that most of us want to know what the future holds. World events seem to be chaotic, terrorism is mushrooming, economic concerns worry us, various nations appear to threaten world peace, and environmental catastrophes appear to be on the horizon. Does the Bible address any of these issues?

It certainly does, but perhaps the Bible discusses them in ways we don't understand.

In the book of Revelation, the last book in the New Testament, numerous prophecies are recorded as taking place in the last years and days of human history. These are calamitous worldwide events that lead up to the second coming of Jesus Christ. The first time Jesus came to earth, he came as a teacher and Savior who died for our sins. The next time he comes to earth will be as a warrior, a ruler, and a judge.

There are a minimum of twenty-one specific major judgments described in Revelation. These depict how God will inflict destruction on the earth—on the lands, seas, trees, grasses, mountains, rivers, islands, cities—and plagues against people who obstinately refuse to turn to God and believe in Christ as their Savior. In just two of these twenty-one judgments taken together, the earth's population is reduced by one-half. Jesus also taught about the same kinds of judgments on earth in the end times. He described a time when humanity would be near extinction. He told his disciples, "For at that [future] time there will be great tribulation, the kind that hasn't taken place from the beginning of the world until now and never will again! Unless those days were limited, no one would survive" (Matthew 24:21–22 HCSB). That sounds like a Doomsday to me.

The Earliest Prophecy of the Return of Christ

Did you know that 25 to 27 percent of the Bible contains predictions, and half of these prophecies have not yet been fulfilled? That means that about one in every twenty-five verses in the New Testament refers to the return of Christ to the earth and the events that accompany the end of history as we know it.

It may be surprising even for Christians who are well-read in the Bible to learn where the first prophecy of the second coming of Christ is found. It is found in Genesis 3:15. Keep in mind that Genesis is the very first book of our Bible. Many Christians understand Genesis 3:15 to be the first prophecy of Christ's *first* coming. This is absolutely true, but the prophecy is fulfilled only partially by Jesus' first coming. Let me explain why. In Genesis 3, Adam and Eve had just committed the first sin of all humanity. The serpent, controlled by Satan, had tempted the first couple to rebel against God.

God came to Eve in the garden of Eden, and began by confronting Satan, who spoke through the serpent. The Lord said, "And I will put enmity between you and the woman [Eve], and between your offspring and hers; he [one of the woman's offspring] will crush your head, and you will strike his heel" (Genesis 3:15 NIV).

The woman's offspring, who would crush the serpent's head, is a prediction of the coming of Jesus as the Messiah, the offspring of a woman (i.e., a person who would be born of a woman and would be fully human). The virgin birth of Jesus fulfills this part of the prophecy. Satan attacked Jesus' "heel," a less vulnerable blow than the blow to the serpent's (Satan's) "head." The blow to the heel of the woman's offspring took place at the cross when the devil worked through humans to bring about the crucifixion of Jesus. The cross is also where Jesus paid the penalty for our sins and began the ultimate lethal attack on the serpent's head.

The first coming of Christ and his death on the cross are not the complete fulfillment of this prophecy. The final and conclusive attack on the head of the serpent will take place as a result of the second coming. It is then that Jesus will cast Satan into the lake of fire to be eternally punished for his evil rebellion and destruction of people's lives (Revelation 20:10). It is not surprising that in Revelation 12:9 and 20:2, Satan is called the "ancient serpent," recalling the work of Satan in the garden of Eden.

How can we be sure Genesis 3:15 is about the second coming of Christ, and not only the first coming? In his letter to the Romans, the apostle Paul made an allusion to Genesis 3:15. He wrote to the Roman Christians (and ultimately, to all believers), "I want you to be *wise in doing right* and to stay innocent of any wrong. The

God of peace *will soon crush Satan* under your feet" (Romans 16:19–20). Paul's reference to being "wise in doing right" recalls Genesis 2:16–17, where God told Adam and Eve not to eat of the Tree of Knowledge of Good and Evil. When Eve was tempted by the serpent in the garden, she "saw that the tree was beautiful and its fruit looked delicious, and she wanted the wisdom it would give her" (Genesis 3:6). She unwisely ate of the forbidden fruit, gave it to her husband to eat, and sin entered the entire human race.

In Romans 16:20, Paul also used the vocabulary of Genesis 3 in the phrase "will soon crush Satan under your feet." The crushing of Satan (the serpent in the garden) by the God of peace will take place soon. The second coming of Christ and all its accompanying events are frequently said to take place "soon." In the closing remarks in the book of Revelation, the apostle John was told, "The Lord, the God who inspires the prophets, sent his angel to show his servants *the things that must soon take place*" (Revelation 22:6 NIV). One of the accompanying events to the second coming of Christ will be the final, complete defeat of Satan.

Jesus the Prophet

I recently taught on prophecy to an adult Bible class and asked, "What titles should we give Jesus?" I received most of the traditional titles: Christ, Messiah, Son of Man, Son of God, Priest, King, Lord, Wonderful Counselor, Almighty God, etc. After numerous titles were suggested, I realized that no one called Jesus Prophet. Perhaps the most neglected title for Jesus is Prophet. In fact, Jesus was the greatest of all the prophets.

I would maintain that to study and pay close attention to yet-to-be-fulfilled prophecies of Jesus and the Bible is to greatly honor Jesus. Some Christians seem to treat his prophecies that have been fulfilled differently from his prophecies that have yet to be fulfilled. Christians often use fulfilled prophecies as proof of the accuracy of the Bible and its inspiration, or as proof of Jesus' deity. We should not forget that these fulfilled prophecies, when Jesus first gave them, were predictions of yet future events just as unfulfilled prophecies are to us today.

Consider some of Jesus' fulfilled prophecies. He regularly predicted his own death. Shortly before his public ministry of approximately three years ever began, Jesus told the Jewish leaders in the temple, "Destroy this temple, and in three days I will raise it up" (John 2:19). They thought Jesus was referring to the physical temple in which they were standing. The apostle John writes, "But when Jesus said 'this temple,' he meant his own body" (v. 21). Jesus was predicting his crucifixion and his resurrection three days later.

Jesus also predicted the kind of death he would die. In John 12, Jesus said, "And when I am lifted up from the earth, I will draw everyone to myself" (v. 32). Then John interpreted Jesus' teaching: "He said this to indicate how he was going to die" (v. 33). He would be lifted up on a Roman cross. Jesus prophesied that Judas, one of his disciples, would betray him (John 13:21, 26). He predicted that Peter would deny him three times before the rooster crowed (Matthew 26:34). He foretold that all the disciples would forsake him (26:31). He prophesied that he had to die in the city of Jerusalem (16:21) and that it had to be during the Passover (26:2). He predicted the coming of the Holy Spirit (John 14:26).

Jesus also predicted events that would come on the Jewish people. He prophesied that the city of Jerusalem would be surrounded by armies and be destroyed (Luke 19:43–44; 21:20). At that same time, the temple would be completely destroyed so that not a single building stone of the temple would remain on top of another (Matthew 24:1–2). Finally, Jesus predicted that the people of Jerusalem would "be killed by the sword or sent away as captives to all the nations of the world. And Jerusalem will be trampled down by the Gentiles until the period of the Gentiles comes to an end" (Luke 21:24).

The fulfillment of these events took place when Titus, a Roman general who would eventually become emperor, led the dominant Roman armies (Gentiles) to besiege Jerusalem and destroy it during the invasions of AD 67–70. Flavius Josephus (born in AD 37/38), a Jewish historian of the time, records that 1,100,000 Jewish people died in the attacks on Jerusalem and 97,000 Jews were taken captive.

Did you notice the last sentence of Luke 21:24: "And Jerusalem will be trampled down by the Gentiles *until* the period of the Gentiles comes to an end"? The little word *until* contains an indirect implication that Jerusalem will not remain under the control of the Gentiles indefinitely. It prophesies a future time when the Jewish people will return to Israel and the period in which the Gentiles will dominate Jerusalem and the land of Israel will end. Some believe this was fulfilled in 1948, when Israel returned to their land as a nation once again. Others understand that this will be fulfilled at the second coming of Christ to the earth. Either way, it is an amazing prediction.

Consider other prophecies of Jesus that are still future. For example, the second longest uninterrupted teaching of Jesus in the New Testament is a prophetic message about the end times (Matthew 24–25). Christians call this teaching the Olivet Discourse because it was a speech or sermon given to Jesus' disciples on the Mount of Olives. The Mount of Olives is a small mountain or hill that overlooks Jerusalem from the city's east side.

Most other famous messages Jesus gave are only found in one of the four gospels of the New Testament. For example, the Sermon on the Mount is found only in Matthew 5–7. This is the message that contains the famous Beatitudes (Matthew 5:3–12). (A sermon in Luke 6 has some similar subjects, but was probably given at a different time.) The Farewell Discourse—a message given in an upstairs room the night before Jesus was crucified—is found only in John 13–17. But the Olivet Discourse has a parallel account in three of the four gospels: Matthew 24–25; Mark 13; and Luke 21. Parts of this message are also found in Luke 17. Jesus' Olivet Discourse in Matthew is the longest of these prophecies. Put together, Jesus' teachings about prophecy are probably given more space in the New Testament than any other subject he taught.

Add to this the fact that Jesus is the one who gave to the apostle John the visions and prophecies of the book of Revelation. The book opens with this statement: "The revelation of Jesus Christ, which God gave him [Jesus] to show to his servants the things that must soon take place" (Revelation 1:1 ESV). Once again, we note that prophecy is the largest subject in Jesus' teachings. And if it is the largest subject, it might also be the most important. That's how significant Bible prophecy is.

Nevertheless, some people, even some Christians, play down the importance of Bible prophecy. They think these teachings are not that essential to proper Christian living or that they cause too much controversy. People like this often comment that the book of Revelation is too difficult to understand and that the differences of interpretation among Christians result in divisiveness. Perhaps they have also known someone who always talks about prophecy and seems to be consumed with this subject as if it were the only topic in the Bible. I understand the barrier to taking prophecy seriously after one has encountered a Christian who is obsessed with Bible prophecy. Such prophecy "authorities" allow their thinking and conversations to be dominated by minutia about the mark of the Beast, or the Antichrist, or the fulfillment of a Bible prophecy in current events. Details of Bible prophecy are important, but fascination or obsession with prophecy misses the real intention for which God gave us glimpses into the future—and that is to point us to who Jesus really is.

The book of Revelation does spend much of its content describing the Antichrist and the False Prophet who works with him. It also describes the final world powers that will gather together in warfare and the final conflict that will result. Bible prophecy tells us that the future evil world ruler called the Antichrist will be the most powerful, most wicked human being who has ever lived—and the most satanically controlled person as well. He will become dictator of the whole world, and people will worship him as God.

The fact that the book of Revelation gives in such detail this description of the power of Satan, the Antichrist, and the False

Prophet is not to satisfy our curiosity or consume our conversations, but to demonstrate how far greater Jesus' ultimate victory will be over all his enemies. He will destroy them with his astounding power and glory when he comes back to earth in holy warfare. As if it were totally effortless for Jesus, Revelation tells us simply that "the beast [the Antichrist] was captured, and with him the false prophet. . . . Both the beast and his false prophet were thrown alive into the fiery lake of burning sulfur" (19:20). The apostle John describes that at a later time Satan will be bound and ultimately punished as well: "The devil . . . was thrown into the fiery lake of burning sulfur, joining the beast and the false prophet" (20:10).

Right before the account of the second coming of Christ in Revelation, the following words are given to the apostle John to write: "For the essence of prophecy is to give a clear witness for Jesus" (Revelation 19:10). Let me restate the verse this way. "The very heart and purpose of prophecy is to point to who Jesus really is." Prophecy demonstrates that Jesus is the most significant, most powerful, most worthy person in the universe.

How Prophecy Motivates Proper Christian Behavior

It may seem surprising at first to learn that nearly all prophetic passages in the Bible are designed to stimulate proper Christian living here on earth. Very few prophecies are given without exhortations to moral and ethical behavior. Here are a few examples of moral, ethical, and practical attitudes and actions that are specifically motivated by prophecy. You may be surprised at a few of the attitudes or actions that are encouraged by prophetic truth.

Comfort:
For the Lord Himself will descend from heaven with a shout, with the voice of the archangel and with the trumpet of God, and the dead in Christ will rise first. Then we who are alive and remain will be caught up together with them in the clouds to meet the Lord in

the air, and so we shall always be with the Lord. Therefore comfort one another with these words.

1 Thessalonians 4:16–18 NASB

Judgmental Spirit:

But why do you judge your brother? Or why do you show contempt for your brother? For we shall all stand before the judgment seat of Christ.

Romans 14:10 NKJV

Generosity:

Command those who are rich in this present world not to be arrogant nor to put their hope in wealth, which is so uncertain, but to put their hope in God, who richly provides us with everything for our enjoyment. Command them to do good, to be rich in good deeds, and to be generous and willing to share. In this way they will lay up treasure for themselves as a firm foundation for the coming age, so that they may take hold of the life that is truly life.

1 Timothy 6:17–19 NIV

Most Christians know Jesus' teaching in Matthew 7:1, even if they don't know the Scripture reference: "Do not judge others." Even many non-Christians know this saying of Jesus—although they usually use it incorrectly to avoid confrontation by someone who suggests that, according to the Bible, their lifestyle is sinful. The whole sentence says, "Do not judge others, and you will not be judged." Did you notice that prophecy is the motivation behind this command? Most of those who can quote this verse don't remember or know the next sentence that further explains the prophecy. "For you will be treated as you treat others. The standard you use in judging is the standard by which you will be judged" (7:2). It seems important that we understand this prophetic truth in order to help us avoid judging others.

How likely are you to judge others, if you understand that the critical, unloving standard you use on them will be used to evaluate you when Christ comes back? This judgment is not the judgment that determines our final destiny in heaven. A chronology of Jesus' ministry in the four gospels shows that when Jesus spoke Matthew 7, he was addressing his disciples who had already believed in him (cf. John 2:11). By this time, all eleven disciples, except Judas (John 13:10–11), had put their faith in Jesus as the true Messiah. So Jesus was teaching about *the judgment seat of Christ*. This term is used in the Bible to describe how each person who has believed in Jesus for eternal life will receive an evaluation for special future rewards. In other words, God will examine each true Christian to determine his or her level of faithfulness as a Christian. This judgment will be discussed more in chapter 12.

2

Are There Signs That We Are in the End Times?

Western history has always had individuals or groups who have prophesied the future. Some are psychics, such as Edgar Cayce (1877–1945) and Jean Dixon (1904–1997). Others are seers who directly practiced the occult, such as Nostradamus (1503–1566). Of particular interest are those who have predicted the return of Christ or the end of the world. A few have been leaders of quasi-Christian groups, such as Herbert W. Armstrong (1892–1986) of the Worldwide Church of God; Charles T. Russell (1852–1916), whose teachings led to the Jehovah's Witnesses sect; and Joseph Smith (1805–1844), founder of the Mormons. Smith implied that Christ would return about 1891. Russell predicted that Christ would return in 1914. When this didn't happen, he claimed that Christ returned secretly but had revealed himself only to Jehovah's Witnesses.

Can Anyone Predict When Jesus Will Come Back?

Unfortunately, even leaders of accepted evangelical Christian traditions have sometimes made similar projections. In 1970,

Hal Lindsey published *The Late Great Planet Earth* and sold 28 million copies. While there were many beneficial teachings in his book, in it he suggested that Christ would return at least by 1988. While the prediction was a very minor part of the book, readers took it seriously. He drew his calculations from a parable in the Olivet Discourse that Jesus told about the fig tree: "When its branches bud and its leaves begin to sprout, you know that summer is near. In the same way, when you see all these things, you can know his return is very near, right at the door" (Matthew 24:32–33). Following the lesson from the fig tree, Jesus promised, "This generation will not pass from the scene until all these things take place" (v. 34).

Lindsey interpreted the fig tree to be a symbol of Israel, and the budding of the fig tree to be a description of Israel's return to its own land and their prosperity that followed. He also understood the statement "This generation will not pass from the scene until all these things take place" as referring to the generation that sees Israel as a nation in their own land again. Israel miraculously became a nation again in 1948 after twenty-five hundred years of control by foreign powers. Lindsey determined from his study of the Bible that, according to the Old Testament, a generation was forty years. So by adding forty years (one generation) to 1948, Jesus had to return sometime before 1988. When he published his book in 1970, he had an eighteen-year window before the prediction was proved wrong.

One of the problems missed in Lindsey's interpretation was that the fig tree parable is also found in Luke 21, a parallel passage to Matthew 24. In the Luke 21 passage, Jesus said, "Notice the fig tree, *or any other tree*" (Luke 21:29). The fig tree does not predict Israel's becoming a nation again. Israel cannot at the same time symbolize the fig tree or any other tree. The parable is simply a lesson from looking at trees in general. When trees visibly bear their leaves in the spring, you know that summer is coming soon. When certain signs appear in the world, you can know that Jesus' return to earth is near.

Another statement of Jesus in the Olivet Discourse is also over-looked whenever someone predicts the future coming of Christ. This statement by Jesus, "Now concerning that day and hour no one knows—neither the angels in heaven, nor the Son—except the Father only" (Matthew 24:36 HCSB), should silence all such attempts to predict or estimate the time of his coming. Jesus was teaching about sudden earthly catastrophes, divine judgments, and other dreadful events that would lead up to and climax at his future return to earth. Like the parable of the fig tree, when this series of events begins, Jesus' return to earth will follow. This is what Christians call the second coming of Christ.

When does this series of events *begin* that signals the end and the return of Jesus to earth? When will these divine judgments start? No one knows when that day or hour will come—the day that worldwide catastrophes begin and lead to the final return of Jesus. Someone once said in good humor, "Only the Father knows, and he ain't tellin'."

Of course, it was only while Jesus was on earth in his humanity and fully submitted to God the Father that he did not know the time these catastrophic events will begin and when he will return. Now in heaven, he fully exercises his deity and certainly knows the time of his own return. No human person can predict when these coming judgments will begin. Even the angels don't know the time of his return for believers, not even Michael the archangel. One would think that if anyone in the universe could figure out when Jesus will come, the angels could figure this out by observing the world events and knowing the prophecies of the Bible.

What Does the Bible Mean by the Coming of Christ?

I have been talking about the second coming of Christ. Actually, the Bible never uses the term *second coming* of Christ. That doesn't mean the term is wrong. The Bible does use terms that *refer to* a future coming of Christ. For example, Jesus told his disciples right before his death, "There are many rooms in my Father's house. I wouldn't tell you this, unless it was true. I am going there to prepare a place for each of you. After I have done this, I will come back and take you with me. Then we will be together" (John 14:2–3 CEV). So Jesus will "come back" to take us to be with him forever.

Let me make some important clarifications about what I mean by the second coming of Christ. As already mentioned, Jesus said, "Now concerning that day and hour no one knows." This statement implies that the time of the coming of Christ cannot be known by any human. Many places in the Bible describe the coming of Christ as a surprise event. The time of its arrival cannot be known. On the other hand, some statements in the Bible imply that Jesus' coming will be very observable and predictable. Various recognizable signs will precede his coming.

In the fig tree parable, Jesus said, "When its [the fig tree's] branches bud and its leaves begin to sprout, *you know* that summer is near. In the same way, when you see all these things [prophesied in Matthew 24:3–31], *you can know* his return is very near, right at the door" (Matthew 24:32–33). According to statements like this one, people can know when Christ's final return to earth will be because his return will be preceded by multiple signs observable to everyone. Doesn't this sound different from Jesus' statement just a few verses later? "Now concerning that day and hour *no one knows* . . ." (Matthew 24:36 HCSB). How can such statements be reconciled?

A solution to this supposed contradiction is not difficult. The word *coming* in the Bible, when speaking of the coming of Christ in the future, is a word that includes various stages and events, not just a single, momentary happening. We often use the word *coming* in this way in normal conversation. I may say, "When my family comes, we will celebrate Thanksgiving together." By that I don't mean the exact moment they arrive at my house. They might arrive on a Tuesday, but we will celebrate Thanksgiving on Thursday. By referring to their coming, I am referring to their visit of several days.

We also speak of the first coming of Christ this way. We may use the term first coming of Christ to refer to the Christmas story, the birth of Jesus. Or we might use the same term to refer to the time when Jesus was crucified, died, and was resurrected. His first coming may have reference to one primary, brief event. At other times, we use the first coming of Christ to refer to everything that happened to Jesus while he was on earth, from his birth to his ascension.

The second coming of Christ in the end times may also be viewed in a way that focuses on a single event or on a series of events, depending on the context. The second coming of Christ involves a series of events with at least two stages. First, Jesus will come in the air (not to the earth) and catch up all the dead and living people who have placed their faith in Jesus. Then he will return with them to heaven.

This event is commonly called the rapture. The passage in John 14 cited on the previous page is describing this event. Those caught up to meet Jesus in the air are only those who have received eternal life through faith in Jesus while on earth. This faith brings a new, spiritual birth and eternal life. Jesus spoke of this new life to a man named Nicodemus in John 3:1–21. This would be an important section of the Bible to read if you are not familiar with it. Jesus called this event being "born again" or "born from above."

Signs Versus No Signs

The rapture, the "catching up" of believers to heaven, is the first stage of the second coming of Christ. This event of believers being caught up to be with Jesus will have no warnings, no telltale signs, not even signs to warn true Christians. It will be totally a surprise event. That's what Jesus was talking about when he said, "But concerning that day and hour no one knows, not even the angels in heaven, nor the Son, but the Father only" (Matthew 24:36 esv). No one knows "that day and hour," i.e., the time when the rapture will take place and the divine judgments immediately following that will come on those left behind. It is a totally unpredictable event. Jesus explained further, "Two men will be working together in the field; one will be taken, the other left. Two women will be grinding flour at the mill; one will be taken, the other left" (Matthew 24:40–41). Those taken will be the ones caught up to meet Jesus in the air. Those left will remain on the earth.

The rapture will be followed immediately by seven years of earthly disasters. This time is commonly called by many Christians the great tribulation. In Jesus' teaching, the ones who are left on earth will go through the divine judgments of this time period. The tribulation is not the normal trials, difficulties, and tribulations Christians go through, but a specific time period. In this book, the tribulation will refer to this future seven-year period of great trauma and tragedy on the earth.

At the very climax of the tribulation, when the whole world will be in radical chaos, Jesus will return to the earth, slowly, physically, and visibly for all to see. This is different from his coming at the rapture. The rapture will be a split second in time. The apostle Paul wrote of the rapture,

> But let me reveal to you a wonderful secret. We will not all die, but we will all be transformed! It will happen in a moment, in the blink of an eye, when the last trumpet is blown. For when the trumpet sounds, those who have died will be raised to live forever. And we who are living will also be transformed [i.e., resurrected]. For our dying bodies must be transformed into bodies that will never die.
>
> 1 Corinthians 15:51–53

When the rapture takes place, it "will happen in a moment, in the blink of an eye" (v. 52). The word *moment* in this passage in the original language of the New Testament is the ancient Greek word *atomos*. We derive our English word *atom* from this word. The atom is the smallest unit of matter. The rapture takes place in the smallest unit of time. When Jesus appeared to others shortly after his resurrection, he appeared only to those who had believed in him. He even "appeared to more than five hundred of the brothers and sisters at one time" (1 Corinthians 15:6 NET). It seems that in a similar way at the rapture, only believers will see Jesus in the air as the resurrected Savior and be caught up to be with him.

This is not the case when Christ returns to earth at the end of the seven years of the tribulation. He will return all the way to earth. Several Bible passages state that everyone in the world will see Jesus coming to earth at this time. Therefore, if everyone can see him descending, it must be a slow event. As Revelation states, "Look! He is returning with the clouds, and every eye will see him, even those who pierced him, and all the tribes on the earth will mourn because of him. This will certainly come to pass! Amen" (Revelation 1:7 NET).

When the apostle John wrote, "even those who pierced him," he was referring to how the Jewish people participated in Jesus' crucifixion. Sometime before Jesus comes back to earth, the majority of Jewish people in the world will realize their error as an ethnic group and will come to faith in Jesus as their Messiah. That's what the statement "and all the [Jewish] tribes on the earth will mourn because of him" means. This mourning will be done in faith, and it will include some from all twelve tribes of the Jewish people.

The Old Testament prophet Zechariah predicted that the Jewish people would turn to their Messiah in faith sometime before they see Jesus returning from heaven. Zechariah recorded that the Lord said, "Then I will pour out a spirit of grace and prayer on the family of David and on the people of Jerusalem. They will look on me [Jesus] whom they have pierced and mourn for him as for an only son. They will grieve bitterly for him as for a firstborn son who has died" (12:10). After Jesus slowly descends to earth, he will immediately destroy all his enemies (which will be much of the world at that time) and begin to rule the world himself. This return of Christ to the earth is the second stage to his second coming. To make things clearer, I will refer to the first stage as the rapture and to this final stage as Christ's return to earth.

The first stage (the rapture and sudden beginning of the tribulation) is an unpredictable event; the second stage is a highly predictable event. The surprise element of the first stage, the rapture, was taught by Jesus in his parables about the coming of a thief in the night. Here is one of those parables. "But understand this: If the owner of the house had known at what time of night the thief was coming, he would have kept watch and would not have let his house be broken into. So you also must be ready, because the Son of Man will come at an hour when you do not expect him" (Matthew 24:43–44 NIV).

The title of this chapter is "Are There Signs That We Are in the End Times?" Perhaps you can now see that the answer to this question depends on what you mean by "the end times." There are no signs that can tell us of the coming of the rapture and the tribulation of seven years that immediately follows the rapture. Once the tribulation starts, it will be exactly seven years later that Christ will come down to earth, visibly and physically. For this second stage, there are *many* signs of Jesus' coming. All of these signs will take place within the tribulation of seven years. The book of Revelation describes at least three groups of seven judgments each (a total of twenty-one judgments) that Christ will send on the earth. These are referred to in the book of Revelation as the seven seal judgments (6:1), the seven trumpet judgments (8:2), and the seven bowl judgments (16:1). As you read Revelation, you will see many other judgments as well.

At the rapture, all those who have received Christ by faith—both the dead and the living—will be caught up to be with Christ. The very next moment after the rapture, everyone on the earth will be an unbeliever—one who has rejected Jesus as his or her personal Savior. These twenty-one judgments are brought on those who have rejected Christ as Messiah. While the majority of the world will remain hardened in unbelief during these seven years, there will still be many who come to faith in Jesus as their Savior. Most of those who come to faith in Jesus during the tribulation will be severely persecuted and many will be martyred for their faith.

In the fourth seal judgment, one-fourth of the people of the world will die (Revelation 6:7–8), and in the sixth trumpet judgment, one-third of the remaining population of earth will die (9:14–15). In just these two judgments of the twenty-one judgments of the tribulation, one-half of the world's population will die. In modern terms, Jesus will not return to the earth until 3 or 4 billion people die within a few years' time. When this happens, will anyone on earth miss such a revealing sign of Christ's return to earth?

Even worse, right before Christ returns to earth, there will be very few survivors on the planet at all. Recall the prophecy of Jesus mentioned earlier. "For at that time there will be great tribulation, the kind that hasn't taken place from the beginning of the world until now and never will again! Unless those days were limited, no one would survive" (Matthew 24:21–22 HCSB).

Several other prophecies specify the time of Christ's return to earth. Jesus said, "And this gospel of the kingdom will be preached in the whole world as a testimony to all nations, and then the end will come" (Matthew 24:14 NIV). Those who research the spread of the message of Christ calculate that approximately thirty-nine hundred people groups have not yet been reached with the truths of the Christian faith. This accounts for approximately 40 percent of all people groups. Will all nations soon be reached with the gospel of the kingdom? Can Jesus return to earth at any moment like a thief in the night?

Are there signs that forecast the time at which Jesus will come in the air for believers and begin the tribulation judgments of Revelation? No! Are there signs that forecast the time at which Jesus will come to the earth? Yes! These latter signs are grouped into two types: prophecies that could be fulfilled before the rapture/tribulation, and prophecies that are to be fulfilled during the tribulation. None of the signs that could be fulfilled before the rapture predict either the exact time of the rapture or the exact time of Jesus' return to earth. If there were a prophecy that predicted that Jesus would come to earth eight years after a certain event, then when that event took place, one could simply subtract the seven years of the tribulation and determine the exact time of the rapture. If such a prophecy existed, it would contradict Jesus' teaching about the surprise arrival of the rapture.

Many Christians point to general signs as evidence of the return of Christ to the earth. These include among others the increase in earthquakes and natural disasters, the ability of mankind to totally annihilate the human race (e.g., as by nuclear weapons), climate change that threatens life on earth, and the rise of radical Islam and ISIS. Also, the Bible pictures a one-world government and economy during the tribulation and the time that directly leads up to Jesus' coming to earth. When we see rising characteristics that may contribute to a one-world government—the increase of global communications, the widespread influence and access of the Internet, and the progress toward a cashless society and a single global economy—then the predicted one-world government and the second coming of Christ come closer and closer. But no one is able to predict the time of the rapture or the second coming of Jesus to the earth by these signs.

The rise of the Antichrist to power must take place before the second coming. Scripture indicates that the Antichrist won't be clearly identifiable by anyone until the tribulation begins. Eventually, he will demand that the whole world worship him. This latter event will begin at the middle of the tribulation, precisely three and a half years before Jesus returns to earth. Once the Antichrist appears, the coming of Christ to earth will be highly predictable. Once the rapture takes place and the tribulation begins, there are many signs that predict the precise time Jesus will return to earth.

Some prophesied events that point to Christ's second coming to earth may find fulfillment before the rapture. Once again, these signs do not indicate the time of Christ's return. An example of this type of prophecy is the prediction that Israel will become a nation again, in its own land. No passage in Scripture directly mentions when this will be fulfilled, whether before or after the rapture. It could have been fulfilled hundreds of years ago or it could be fulfilled shortly after the rapture. Ultimately, this prophecy was fulfilled in 1948, when the Jewish people were restored to the land of Israel as a nation. This is not a sign of the rapture, but it is a sign of the final return of Christ to the earth. Prophecy only indicates that the Jewish people will be a nation once again no later than early in the tribulation.

As we will see later, the prophet Daniel predicts that the ancient Roman Empire will be revived sometime before Jesus returns to earth. This has not happened yet. It may happen long before the rapture or it may take place shortly after the rapture. But the ancient Roman Empire must be revived by the early stages of the tribulation, and therefore is a sign of Jesus' return to earth.

I once heard this illustration: "When you see Christmas decorations coming out in all the stores and shopping malls, you know that Thanksgiving is right around the corner." The decorations in the stores are signs of Christmas, not of Thanksgiving. When we see the signs of Christmas, we know that Thanksgiving is soon to come. When we see signs of the final return of Christ to the earth, we know that the rapture is coming closer and closer. No one can accurately predict the day or hour or even year of the rapture and the coming tribulation.

Another prophecy in Scripture that illustrates this truth is the prophecy that the Jewish temple in Jerusalem must be rebuilt. Various passages clearly picture this temple in Jerusalem at least by the midpoint of the future seven-year tribulation. Of course, this prophecy has not yet been fulfilled. It is not a sign of the rapture but of the return of Christ to the earth. It could be accomplished several years into the seven-year tribulation, or it could be accomplished many years before the rapture and the tribulation begin. Regardless, it is a sign of the return of Christ to the earth, not a sign of the coming of Christ in the rapture of believers.

Are We Living in the Last Days?

The Bible does seem to teach that the world is continuing to get worse and worse. Even now, the world is progressing toward greater evil and wickedness. In fact, sometimes the Bible speaks of the last days as the whole time since Jesus left this earth. Jesus' first coming was a turning point in God's work in the world. The world is moving rapidly to the climax of its history. From that perspective, the last two thousand years are the last days. The following words were written by the apostle Paul to his young disciple Timothy. They describe the last days as the whole time since Jesus left this earth.

> But mark this: There will be terrible times in the last days. People will be lovers of themselves, lovers of money, boastful, proud, abusive, disobedient to their parents, ungrateful, unholy, without love, unforgiving, slanderous, without self-control, brutal, not lovers of the good, treacherous, rash, conceited, lovers of pleasure rather than lovers of God—having a form of godliness but denying its power.
>
> 2 Timothy 3:1–5 NIV

The Lesson of the Question
"Are There Signs That We Are in the End Times?"

Edgar Whisenant, a retired NASA engineer, published a book in 1988 called *88 Reasons Why the Rapture Will Be in 1988*. The book sold 4.5 million copies. He was fully aware of Jesus' statement in Matthew 24:36 that no one knows the "day or hour" of Christ's return. Yet Whisenant insisted that this did not preclude faithful followers from knowing the year, the month, or the week of the Lord's return. Surely this misses the intention of Jesus' statement.

In 1997, Ed Dobson, a pastor of an evangelical megachurch in Grand Rapids, Michigan, wrote *The End: Why Jesus Could Return by A.D. 2000* (Zondervan). The title states, *Why Jesus Could Return by A.D. 2000,* not *Why Jesus Will Return by A.D. 2000.* That doesn't excuse the charge of date-setting. As is obvious, Jesus didn't come that year. In 2001, Harold Camping, a Bible teacher and manager of a Christian radio network, began to teach that the rapture would take place on May 21, 2011. This was far more specific than Hal Lindsey's or Ed Dobson's prediction. When the rapture did not occur on that date, Camping recalculated Christ's return to be October 21, 2011 instead. After his second prediction also proved erroneous, he acknowledged his error. Christian leaders who refuted Camping's claim repeatedly cited Jesus' clear statement of Matthew 24:36. Yet we are continuing to hear, and will continue to hear, of Christian authors, preachers, and televangelists who predict or imply a date for the Lord's return.

Don't think that you or anyone else can predict or estimate even the decade of Christ's return. One cannot determine the year, month, week, day, or hour when a thief might come. Thieves don't give telltale signs or warnings of their coming. So it is with Jesus' coming at the rapture. He gave the following parable with this warning in mind:

> The coming of the Son of Man can be illustrated by the story of a man going on a long trip. When he left home, he gave each of his slaves instructions about the work they were to do, and he told the gatekeeper to watch for his return.
>
> You, too, must keep watch! For you don't know when the master of the household will return—in the evening, at midnight, before dawn, or at daybreak. Don't let him find you sleeping when he arrives without warning. I say to you what I say to everyone: Watch for him!
>
> Mark 13:34–37

3

What Is the Tribulation?

I've heard some skeptics and even some Christians say something like this: "The God of the Old Testament is so bloody, so harsh, so unloving. But the God of the New Testament is all about love. The God of the Old Testament and the God of the New Testament seem to be a contradiction!" This statement is quite surprising (and untruthful), especially if the skeptics have ever read the whole Bible thoroughly. The Old Testament frequently speaks of the God of Israel as a merciful and loving God. King David of Israel authored Psalm 23, the most cherished of all the 150 individual psalms. He wrote of God, "Surely your goodness and unfailing love will pursue me all the days of my life" (Psalm 23:6). The special Hebrew word for *unfailing love* is used more than 250 times in the Old Testament.

The New Testament certainly reveals the full understanding of the love of God through the crucifixion of Christ on a Roman cross. He suffered a criminal's death to pay the penalty for our sins. The physical pain he suffered was nothing compared with the pain of his separation from God the Father when the sin of the world was placed on him. At that very moment, the agony of that separation was beyond our comprehension. It was precisely at that same moment that Jesus cried out, "My God, my God, why have you abandoned me?" (Matthew 27:46). Right before his death, Jesus said to his disciples, "There is no greater love than to lay down one's life for one's friends" (John 15:13). While all religious groups talk about love, only the Christian faith has a leader who sacrificially modeled what love is.

What is mostly overlooked by skeptics is that God's judgment on sin in the New Testament is as severe as his judgment on sin in the Old Testament. Romans 11:22 says, "Notice how God is both kind and severe." One side is love and mercy; the other side is holiness and justice. Both are themes in the book of Revelation. There is just as much bloodshed by Jesus' judgments in the book of Revelation as there is by God's judgments in the Old Testament. Here is an example from Revelation: "So the angel swung his sickle over the earth and loaded the grapes into the great winepress of God's wrath. The grapes were trampled in the winepress outside the city, and blood flowed from the winepress in a stream about 180 miles long and as high as a horse's bridle" (14:19–20).

As some still do today, ancient peoples threw grapes into a large hewn stone winepress and trampled them by foot to produce juice for wine. The juice ran out the bottom of the winepress through a duct into a lower basin. The grapes in the imagery of Revelation 14 are a symbol of rebellious people, and the grape juice nauseously pictures human blood. This judgment will involve the destruction of human life in the world's last military warfare. This warfare will be a battle to prevent the coming Christ from ruling on earth as king over the world (for more details, see chapter 9 of this book). The 180 miles is roughly the length of the nation of Israel, where this battle will occur. Keep in mind also that the people involved will be the ones who have absolutely refused to repent, even after many years of divine earthly judgments have come on them. Revelation 9:21 states, "They did not repent of their murders or their witchcraft or their sexual immorality or their thefts." The book of Revelation makes this comment or a similar one a total of four times.

The "Day of the Lord" Is a Time of Judgment Like the Flood

The people of the world as a whole think that everything has proceeded for many, many years without a severe divine judgment from heaven. They are convinced that life on earth will continue without God's intervention. The apostle Peter wrote,

> Most importantly, I want to remind you that in the last days scoffers will come, mocking the truth and following their own desires. They will say, "What happened to the promise that Jesus is coming again? . . ."
>
> They deliberately forget that God made the heavens long ago by the word of his command, and he brought the earth out from the water and surrounded it with water. . . . The Lord isn't really being slow about his promise, as some people think. No, he is being patient for your sake. He does not want anyone to be destroyed, but wants everyone to repent. But the day of the Lord will come as unexpectedly as a thief.
>
> 2 Peter 3:3–5, 9–10

God doesn't really want to destroy people. He wants them to come to repentance. That is why he has held off these end-time global judgments as long as he has. Peter reminds his readers that scoffers who reject the possibility of divine, end-time judgments had also purposefully rejected the existence of the flood judgment in Noah's day.

Peter explained that the day of the Lord will come "as unexpectedly as a thief." As we have seen, Jesus used the image of a thief coming at night to illustrate the surprise arrival of the rapture and the beginning of divine judgments on the earth. Peter was drawing on Jesus' teachings from his prophecies in the Olivet Discourse. For Peter and for Jesus, the coming tribulation judgments were like the surprise arrival of the flood in Noah's day.

Jesus told his disciples, "When the Son of Man returns, it will be like it was in Noah's day. In those days before the flood, the people were enjoying banquets and parties and weddings right up to the time Noah entered his boat. People didn't realize what was going to happen until the flood came and swept them all away. That is the way it will be when the Son of Man comes" (Matthew 24:37–39). In Luke 17, Jesus added that the days of Lot also illustrated the surprise arrival of the day of the Lord. In the days of Lot, "People went about their daily business—eating and drinking, buying and selling, farming and building—until the morning Lot left Sodom. Then fire and burning sulfur rained down from heaven and destroyed them all" (vv. 28–29).

The book of Genesis explains that God brought the flood because he "saw that the earth had become corrupt and was filled with violence" (Genesis 6:11). But the lifestyles of pleasure and ease without regard for God were the root causes of their sin. Similarly, the Old Testament city of Sodom was destroyed because of its sin of homosexuality. The root sins were their love of ease and comfort with a disregard for God. "Sodom's sins were pride, gluttony, and laziness, while the poor and needy suffered outside her door" (Ezekiel 16:49). Both the days of Noah and the days of Lot portray the days that lead up to the unpredictable destructions that come suddenly at the start of the day of the Lord or tribulation period.

The Day of the Lord Is Like a Woman in Labor

In the Old Testament, "the day of the Lord" was originally used of any time God brought judgment in his dealings with people on earth. Eventually, the phrase was used of a future time of judgment. The prophets frequently prophesied the coming, future day of the Lord. The description is not pleasant. It is a time when God will finally bring his judgment on earth for its sins against his love and righteousness.

> Scream in terror, for the day of the LORD has arrived—the time for the Almighty to destroy. Every arm is paralyzed with fear. Every heart melts, and people are terrified. Pangs of anguish grip them,

like those of *a woman in labor*. . . . For see, the day of the Lord is coming—the terrible day of his fury and fierce anger. The land will be made desolate, and all the sinners destroyed with it.

"I, the Lord, will punish the world for its evil and the wicked for their sin. . . . I will make people scarcer than gold. . . . For I will shake the heavens. The earth will move from its place when the Lord of Heaven's Armies displays his wrath in the day of his fierce anger."

Isaiah 13:6–9, 11–13

Like this message from the Old Testament prophet Isaiah, many prophecies compare the day of the Lord to a woman in labor. This is because a pregnant woman's labor pains come as a sudden, unannounced event. Even in modern medicine, a precise method of predicting in advance the exact day and hour of a woman's labor are still unknown. The imagery of a woman in labor is much like the thief imagery that Jesus used. Both describe the day of the Lord coming as an unannounced event.

It is not at all surprising that Jesus also mentioned the image of a woman in labor in his Olivet Discourse. Jesus had just told his disciples that the Jerusalem temple would be completely destroyed. Assuming this meant the end of the age, the disciples asked Jesus two questions: "Tell us, when will these things happen? And what is the sign of Your coming and of the end of the age?" (Matthew 24:3 HCSB).

Jesus began his message by warning them of false messiahs that would deceive many people. He also predicted military wars in which "nation will rise up against nation, and kingdom against kingdom" and that "famines and earthquakes" would take place "in various places" (Matthew 24:7 HCSB). In a parallel passage, he added "plagues" or the sudden outbreak of serious diseases (Luke 21:11). Then he summarized these predictions: "All these events are the beginning of birth pains" (Matthew 24:8 HCSB). The phrase *birth pains* gives us the clue that Jesus was referring to the beginning of the day of the Lord or the tribulation period.

The Day of the Lord and the Seventieth Week of Daniel

The tribulation and the day of the Lord are also parallel to the Seventieth Week of Daniel. The prophecy of the Seventy Weeks in Daniel 9:24–27 is one of the most remarkable, long-range predictions in the entire Bible. In fact, it is the most precise prophecy concerning the date of the Messiah's first coming, even specifying the exact year of the Messiah's crucifixion. Then quickly the prophecy jumps to the final drama of human history and describes the last seven years that lead up to the return of Jesus to the earth. The prophecy of the Seventy Weeks is also one of the most challenging to understand, especially if it is the first time one has been exposed to this prophecy. You may want to read the following sections twice.

Daniel 9:27 is the only Old Testament passage mentioned directly by Jesus in his great prophecy in the Olivet Discourse. That should give us an important guideline for understanding this prophetic passage in Matthew. Jesus taught his disciples, "So when you see the abomination that causes desolation, spoken of by the prophet Daniel, standing in the holy place (let the reader understand)..." (24:15 HCSB). When Jesus called for the reader to have understanding or wisdom, he was referring to the reader of the book of Daniel. The next time you read Daniel, underline how often Daniel and his three friends are said to speak or act in wisdom and understanding. Knowledge of the Bible's truth about the end times brings godly wisdom in life. (The "abomination that causes desolation" will be discussed in chapter 6.)

The prophecy begins with the angel Gabriel (Daniel 9:21) explaining to Daniel, "Seventy weeks are decreed about your people and your holy city" (v. 24 HCSB). In place of the words *seventy weeks,* some Bible versions help the reader by translating the phrase as "seventy sevens" (NIV) or simply "a period of seventy sets of seven" (NLT). This is because the word *week* in the original Old Testament Hebrew language does not mean a week of days but just a group of seven. They are actually groups of seven *years,* not seven days.

Shortly after creation, the Old Testament instructs the Jews to arrange seven days for one week with the seventh day as a Sabbath, a day for rest. Later, they were also commanded to group their years into seven-year segments (forty-nine years) with the fiftieth year as a sabbatical year (Leviticus 25:8). Just as the Sabbath, every seventh day, was a day of rest, the sabbatical year required that the Jewish people allow their land to rest and to remain unused. God promised to supply the Jewish people with all the food they needed for the seventh year during the previous six years.

In Daniel 9, Daniel describes how he was praying about the captivity he and other Jews had endured for seventy years in Babylon. He was also reading how the prophet Jeremiah had said that God would punish Israel for her sins. The reason why Israel was captured and exiled to Babylon was because the Israelites refused to obey the sabbatical years. Every seventh year for 490 years, the Jewish people did not allow their land to rest. That amounted to a total of seventy sabbatical years in which the land did not have its rest. Ironically, God himself caused the land to rest for seventy years by taking his people off the land and exiling them to another country, Babylon. Jeremiah predicted this would happen. "So the message of the LORD spoken through Jeremiah was fulfilled. The land finally enjoyed its Sabbath rest, lying desolate until the seventy years were fulfilled, just as the prophet had said" (2 Chronicles 36:21).

God also promised the Jewish people, "You will be in Babylon for seventy years. But then I will come and do for you all the good things I have promised, and I will bring you home again" (Jeremiah 29:10). Daniel was reading this promise of restoration recorded in Jeremiah (Daniel 9:2). In response to Daniel's prayer, the angel Gabriel appeared to him (Daniel 9:21) for the second time in the book (cf. 8:16) and revealed to him the prophecy of the Seventy Weeks. Gabriel appears only two other times in the Bible, both to announce the birth and first coming of the Messiah (Luke 1:19, 26). It is not surprising in Daniel 9 that Gabriel gives a prophecy of the Messiah.

First, notice that the prophecy is specifically about the Jewish people and their city, Jerusalem. It is not about the New Testament church composed of mostly Gentiles who believe in Jesus as their

41

personal Messiah. Gabriel told Daniel, "Seventy weeks [490 years] are decreed about your people and your holy city—to bring the rebellion to an end, to put a stop to sin, to wipe away iniquity, to bring in everlasting righteousness, to seal up vision and prophecy, and to anoint the most holy place" (Daniel 9:24 HCSB).

Like the violation of the sabbatical years that lasted 490 years in the past, the Seventy Weeks prophecy describes a future 490-year period (seventy groups of seven years). Gabriel explained further, "Know and understand this: From the issuing of the decree to restore and rebuild Jerusalem until Messiah the Prince will be seven weeks and sixty-two weeks [a total of sixty-nine weeks]. . . . After those sixty-two weeks, the Messiah will be cut off and will have nothing" (9:25–26 HCSB). Notice the command to Daniel to have knowledge and understanding (wisdom) (v. 25). The command to gain wisdom will also be part of the message of the book of Revelation. The phrase "the Messiah will be cut off" (v. 26) is a reference to the crucifixion of Jesus.

The beginning point of these 490 prophetic years is "from the issuing of the decree to restore and rebuild Jerusalem," and the first sixty-nine weeks (the first 483 years) would be "until Messiah the Prince" comes, i.e., until Jesus comes. The decree that fits best the description of the prophecy of Gabriel is the decree of the Persian king Artaxerxes (Nehemiah 2:1–8) in 444 BC (his twentieth year of reign). The Persians conquered Babylon in 539 BC while Daniel was probably in his eighties. The beginning point for the fulfillment of this prophecy took place many years after Daniel died.

Daniel's Seventieth Week
(Daniel 9:24–27)

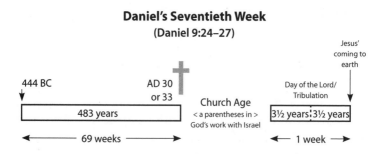

Gabriel revealed to Daniel that it would take seven "weeks" (forty-nine years) to complete the reconstruction of Jerusalem (9:25 HCSB). Then after another sixty-two weeks—or after a total of sixty-nine weeks or 483 years—the Messiah would be "cut off" (v. 26 HCSB). Many who have studied the chronology of Jesus' life have concluded that the most accurate date both historically and biblically for the crucifixion of Jesus is AD 33. Daniel 9:25–26 is a specific prophecy of the precise date that the Messiah will be crucified ("cut off"), i.e., after 483 years (from 444 BC to AD 33).

Daniel and other prophets sometimes used what is called the "prophetic year," i.e., in prophecy they rounded their years off to 360 days instead of the scientific calculation of 365.24 days per year. (By the way, the Jewish people were not scientifically ignorant. Most ancient cultures, including the Jews, knew to adjust their calendars in a similar way as we do when we add a day to the month of February during leap years.)

After making some minor adjustments to our modern calendars that work on 365 days per year, the 483 years bring us precisely from 444 BC to AD 33. Even more amazing is the fact that many Christian interpreters are convinced that the 483 years end precisely on Palm Sunday, AD 33. On this day, just seven days before his crucifixion, Jesus rode into Jerusalem on a donkey to present himself as Messiah and King (Matthew 21:1–11).

Calculating When the Messiah Is "Cut Off"
(Daniel 9:26)

Prophetic Years		Solar Years	
483	years	173,880	days
−444	BC	÷360.24	days
39	AD	476	years
483	years	476	years
×360		−444	BC
173,880	days	32	AD +1 (from 1 BC to 1 AD)
		33	AD

The 483 years leaves a final seven-year period (one "week") that follows Jesus' death. What can account for those last seven years? Nothing in the early church of the book of Acts can adequately account for these final seven years.

The sixty-nine weeks bring us to a dramatic climax—the Messiah's first coming and his death on the cross. The climax of the last week (and the entire Seventy Weeks prophecy) should have an equally climactic ending centered on the Messiah. If the first 483 years bring us precisely to AD 33, adding the last seven years brings us to the date of AD 40. Nothing significant in the history of the Jews or the early Christian church happened in AD 40.

What Is Telescoping?

Since there is no adequate explanation for a past or present fulfillment of the final seven years of Daniel's Seventy Weeks prophecy, this period must still be in the future. That means that a parenthesis or gap of time takes place between the end of the sixty-nine weeks and the Seventieth Week. This is in harmony with numerous prophetic passages that place two predictions together in one verse or sentence, but these two prophecies are ultimately fulfilled at separate times. This pattern of prophecy is often called "telescoping." This suggests that one prophecy is given, but then the author looks far into the future (as with a telescope) and predicts a second but related prophecy.

Compare the prophecy from Isaiah cited by Jesus in Luke 4:16–21. Jesus was speaking in the synagogue at Nazareth. Isaiah reads (the Messiah is speaking), "The Spirit of the Lord God is on Me . . . to proclaim the year of the LORD's favor, and the day of our God's vengeance" (Isaiah 61:1–2 HCSB). When Jesus read this verse to the people in the synagogue, he stopped after the clause "to proclaim the year of the LORD's favor." In fact, Jesus stopped in the middle of a sentence. Luke tells us that at this point Jesus rolled up the scroll and said to the crowd, "The Scripture you've just heard has been fulfilled this very day!" (Luke 4:21).

44

Why did Jesus stop in the middle of the sentence? Because as Jesus spoke, the fulfillment of the favorable year of the Lord was already under way. By God's mercy and grace, Jesus would die on the cross for the sins of all people. But "the day of our God's vengeance" was in the distant future. That day would be fulfilled in the tribulation period. It awaits the future Seventieth Week of Daniel, the seven years of the end times. The two clauses of Isaiah 61:2 are now separated by over two thousand years.

Telescoping can be compared to a person walking down the street of a large city. As he stares up at the skyscrapers, he sees a wide, tall building with a more narrow part of the building extending from the top. When he walks several more blocks and observes the building from another angle, he realizes that the top structure he saw was actually another, taller building. In his first line of sight, the second building appears to be part of the first. From his new viewpoint, he can see that the second building is separated from the first by a street.

Similarly, many Bible prophecies may have two elements that are found together in the same verse or verses, but their fulfillments may come in stages. A parentheses or gap of time splits the two prophecies. So it is with Daniel 9:24–27. Just as the first 483 years of the Daniel 9 prediction leads up to Christ's first coming, so the last seven years will lead up to Christ's second coming to earth.

The Two Halves of the Seventieth Week

Daniel 9 divides the last seven years of the 490-year prophecy into two equal parts of three and a half years each. It also describes the coming wicked world ruler called the Antichrist who will make a treaty with the Jewish people of the future.

> The people of the coming prince will destroy the city and the sanc-
> tuary. . . . He [the coming prince] will make a firm covenant with
> many for one week, but in the middle of the week he will put a stop
> to sacrifice and offering. And the abomination of desolation will

be on a wing of the temple until the decreed destruction is poured out on the desolator.

vv. 26–27 HCSB

The fulfillment of the first part of this prophecy came more than six hundred years after Daniel died. It was the Roman army that destroyed the city of Jerusalem and its temple in AD 70. The "people of the coming prince" are the Romans. According to Daniel's prophecy, the Messiah must be "cut off" or killed (v. 25) before the destruction of Jerusalem in AD 70 (v. 26). This has been fulfilled just as Daniel prophesied.

The "coming prince" (v. 26) is the Antichrist. The wording "the people of the coming prince" implies that the Antichrist will come sometime *after* his people destroy Jerusalem. From other prophecies, we know that his appearance is still to come. The Bible also predicts elsewhere that the vestiges of the old Roman Empire will be resurrected and that the Roman Empire will have significant power over the world in the end times. This coming prince will rise up out of the Roman Empire II to become the Antichrist—the most wicked, evil person who has ever lived. In the tribulation or Seventieth Week of Daniel—the future seven years of Daniel 9—the Antichrist will eventually rule the entire world as a dictator. (For further discussion, see chapter 6.)

In Old Testament times, Israel often signed treaties with pagan nations to assure their protection and safety rather than trusting in God. Israel will do the same in the tribulation. The Antichrist will make a firm or forceful covenant of peace with many in the Israeli leadership. The treaty will be for seven years and probably will include rights for the Jews to offer sacrifices in their rebuilt temple in Jerusalem. This treaty compelled by the Antichrist marks the beginning of the seven years—the beginning of the Seventieth Week of Daniel. But "in the middle of the week" (v. 27), or at the three-and-a-half-year mark, the Antichrist will put a stop to sacrifice and offering in the rebuilt Jerusalem temple. Then the abomination of desolation

46

(or the "abomination that causes desolation") will be set up in the Jerusalem temple. From Jesus' teachings and the book of Revelation, we know that this abomination of desolation will include a statue of the Antichrist that the whole world will be required to worship.

What Is the Time of Jacob's Distress?

Not only will the Antichrist stop Jewish worship from taking place in their rebuilt Jerusalem temple, he will begin an anti-Semitic campaign that will attempt to annihilate all Jews, especially those who have come to faith in Jesus as their Messiah. This begins at the midpoint of the tribulation, halfway through the Seventieth Week. Jeremiah called that day a "time of distress for Jacob." The name *Jacob* stands for the Jewish people because Jacob's twelve sons formed the twelve tribes that constituted the Jewish nation.

> Thus says the LORD: "We have heard a cry of panic, of terror, and no peace. Ask now, and see, can a man bear a child? Why then do I see every man with his hands on his stomach like a woman in labor? Why has every face turned pale? Alas! That day is so great there is none like it; it is a time of distress for Jacob; yet he shall be saved out of it."
>
> 30:5–7 ESV

Since Jeremiah suggested that the time about which he is speaking can be compared to a woman in labor, we can conclude he is speaking about the future tribulation. The prophet also called this time Jacob's distress. This is a time of difficulty to which there is no comparison ("there is none like it"). How many times can be described as "there is none like it"? The simple answer is, only one. Whenever the Bible speaks in various places of a time that is unique, we can know that these passages are speaking of the same occasion—the tribulation.

For example, notice what was told to Daniel in a vision:

> At that time Michael, the archangel who stands guard over your nation, will arise. Then there will be a time of anguish [for Daniel's nation] greater than any since nations first came into existence. But at that time every one of your people whose name is written in the book will be rescued.
>
> 12:1

Michael the archangel is specifically assigned to protect the Jewish people. There will be a time of anguish for them "greater than any since nations first came into existence." This must be the time of Jacob's distress as described by Jeremiah, but the Jewish people who have come to faith in Jesus as their Messiah will be rescued at the end of that distress.

How long is Jacob's distress, or how long is the time of anguish for the Jewish people (Daniel 12:1)? A little later in Daniel's vision, he was told the answer: "It will go on for a time, times, and half a time. When the shattering of the holy people has finally come to an end, all these things will have happened" (12:7). A "time" is one year, "times" is two years, and "half a time" is a half year—a total of three and a half years. So Jacob's distress is precisely three and one half years—the second half of the seven-year tribulation.

What Is the Great Tribulation?

This second half of the Seventieth Week is also called the great tribulation. This is confirmed by Jesus when he mentions this term in his prophetic teachings of the Olivet Discourse. "For at that time there will be great tribulation, the kind that hasn't taken place from the beginning of the world until now and never will again!" (Matthew 24:21–22 HCSB). Jesus was alluding to Daniel 12:7. Again, the time he is discussing is unique: "the kind that hasn't taken place from the beginning of the world until now and never will again!" We can harmonize Matthew 24:21 with

Daniel 12:1, 7 and Jeremiah 30:7. Jesus called this time "great tribulation."

The Antichrist will intensify his persecution of the Jews and all true believers during the final three and a half years of the tribulation. Revelation refers to the great tribulation as a time when many believers will be martyred for their faith. An angel pointed out to John a group of people in heaven standing before God. John was told, "These are the ones who died in the great tribulation" (Revelation 7:14).

This final seven-year tribulation and its division into two halves is mentioned specifically by its length in four different ways. We have seen it mentioned as "one week," as "in the middle" of the week (Daniel 9:27), and as a "time, times, and half a time" (Daniel 7:25; 12:7; Revelation 12:14). It is also referred to as 1,260 days (Revelation 11:3; 12:6) and forty-two months (Revelation 11:2; 13:5). Keep in mind that the 1,260 days is using a "prophetic year" of thirty days for each month. These multiple terms for the three and a half years of the tribulation appear in seven different Bible passages and two different Bible books. It must play a significant role in prophecy. We'll see many of these terms again.

4

Will Christians Be Raptured and Escape the Tribulation?

Left Behind is the title of the first in a series of ten novels by Jerry B. Jenkins and Tim LaHaye. The books have sold more than 65 million copies, with seven books reaching the *New York Times* bestseller list. Four different movies were made based on the novels. The books describe through a storyline the rapture of true Christians and the results for those left on earth to endure the tribulation. I highly recommend the books. Since the genre is fiction, keep in mind that many details are not part of the actual prophecies of the Bible. For example, when the rapture takes place in the novels, the clothes of all who have believed in Christ drop in a heap on the very spot where those people were the moments before the rapture. This is a logical deduction from the fact that these Christians are caught up and resurrected in a split second while ascending to meet Christ. On the other hand, the Bible says nothing about what happens to the clothes of those who are raptured.

Many denominations and churches do not really talk much about the rapture. Perhaps they are seeking to avoid controversy.

This is an admirable motive. Seeking to avoid controversy while seeking to understand prophecy is possible.

It seems best that we sincerely attempt to understand what Paul meant in the primary passage on the rapture, 1 Thessalonians 4:13–17. Paul first visited Thessalonica, the capital of the Roman province of Macedonia (modern Greece), in AD 49. First-century Roman cities were not as small as some of us might think. Thessalonica had a population of about two hundred thousand.

Paul's Teaching About the Rapture in 1 Thessalonians 4

On his first visit to Thessalonica, Paul won many idolatrous people in the city to faith in Jesus Christ. Although Paul stayed there only about three months, he taught them many important Christian truths. These important truths included Bible prophecy. Some of us might think that teaching new converts about Bible prophecy would be inappropriate. The apostle Paul didn't think so. He didn't wait until they were more mature to teach them about prophecy.

He also had a very practical concern in teaching them about the rapture. It was to offer them comfort in their grief over the loss of their Christian friends and relatives. The basic problem for the Thessalonians seemed to be this: In the months since Paul left Thessalonica, some of the believers among the new church there had died. The remaining Christians wondered, "Will these deceased Christian friends miss the blessing of the rapture?" "If Jesus comes soon to catch up living believers, will the bodies of my dead Christian friends and loved ones remain in the grave until sometime later?" Paul wrote a letter back to these believers to help answer these questions. In it, he said,

> And now, dear brothers and sisters, we want you to know what will happen to the believers who have died so you will not grieve like people who have no hope. For since we believe that Jesus died and was raised to life again, we also believe that when Jesus returns, God will bring back with him the believers who have died. We tell

you this directly from the Lord: We who are still living when the Lord returns will not meet him ahead of those who have died.

1 Thessalonians 4:13–15

Paul made it clear that there was no disadvantage for those Christians who have already died. He also claimed that his teaching on the rapture came "directly from the Lord." Some interpreters think this may mean Paul received some divinely inspired knowledge by revelation directly from the Lord. Paul certainly did receive many biblical truths this way. But I understand Paul to be referencing the teachings of Jesus in the Olivet Discourse. Jesus taught about the rapture. Paul was drawing on the prophetic teachings given by Christ, just as all the other apostles did.

Paul wrote his first letter to the Thessalonians in AD 50. Yet he sensed that it was possible that he himself would be alive to experience the rapture. This is why he said, "*We* who are still living when the Lord returns." Since the rapture could happen at any time, including in Paul's own lifetime, the apostle could include himself among those who would be alive when the rapture took place.

In a previous chapter, we learned that the role of Michael the archangel was to protect the Jewish people (Daniel 12:1). Since *archangel* means chief angel, there is only one archangel. The only one who is called an archangel in Scripture is Michael (Jude 9). Paul described the initiation of the rapture like this: "For the Lord himself will come down from heaven with a commanding shout, with the voice of the archangel, and with the trumpet call of God. First, the believers who have died will rise from their graves" (1 Thessalonians 4:16).

According to Paul, Michael assists Christ in initiating the rapture. We also saw in Daniel 12 that he initiates his role of protector of the Jewish people at the very onset of the tribulation. Once the tribulation begins, God will return to working with Israel once again. This may suggest that the rapture and the beginning of the tribulation will occur at approximately the same time. Both are surprise events with no preceding signs. So it is understandable to see that the rapture takes place with the voice of Michael the archangel.

At the rapture, immediately after deceased believers have been raised up and their bodies transformed (resurrected), living believers will be transformed and both groups will meet Christ in the air in their resurrected bodies. Paul says it this way: "Then, together with them, we who are still alive and remain on the earth will be caught up in the clouds to meet the Lord in the air. Then we will be with the Lord forever. So encourage each other with these words" (1 Thessalonians 4:17–18).

The word *rapture* is not actually found in any English version of the Bible. The English word *rapture* comes from a Latin word that means to "snatch away" or "carry off." This Latin word for *rapture* is used in 1 Thessalonians 4:17 in the Latin translation of the New Testament composed about AD 400. In contemporary language, we use the word *rapture* more often to mean "the state of being carried away by intense joyful emotion." In common Christian teaching, the rapture refers to the coming of Christ to carry away or catch up believers to meet him in the air and take them with him to heaven.

This idea of being "caught up" is based on the apostle Paul's use of the original ancient Greek word in 1 Thessalonians 4:17. This Greek word is also used in Acts 8:39. Philip, an early leader and evangelist in the Jerusalem church, was explaining about the Messiah to a governmental official from Ethiopia. This official was a eunuch who had visited Jerusalem and was on his way back home. After the official believed in Jesus as his Savior and was baptized, "the Spirit of the Lord *snatched* Philip *away*. The eunuch never saw him again." Moments later, Philip "found himself farther north at the town of Azotus" (v. 40). In a split second Philip was transported to another place, ten or fifteen miles (16 or 24 km) away. In a similar way, the rapture means believers are snatched away to meet Christ in the air.

So again, in a future unrevealed moment of time, the spirits of believers who have already died (and been in the presence of

Jesus in heaven), by Jesus' power, will miraculously unite with the dust particles of their bodies being raised up from the grave, and join the living believers as they are caught up alive from the earth. That's the rapture. No wonder Paul concluded this prophecy, "So encourage each other with these words" (1 Thessalonians 4:18).

Paul's Teaching About the Rapture in 1 Thessalonians 5

Some books, lectures, or sermons begin with a theme or even an outline of what is about to be said or written. The table of contents in a book gives such an overview. Some Bible books also do something like this. In the introduction to his first letter to the Thessalonians, Paul gave an overview of what he was about to say to the new church at Thessalonica. In 1 Thessalonians 1:9–10, he described how people throughout the Roman provinces kept talking about the radical transformation in the lives of these new Christians: "For they themselves report what kind of reception we had from you: how you turned to God from idols to serve the living and true God and to wait for His Son from heaven, whom He raised from the dead—Jesus, who rescues us from the coming wrath" (HCSB).

These verses are the outline for what Paul will write in his letter. The reception that Paul received is discussed more fully in chapters 2–4. In 1 Thessalonians 4:13–18, Paul began to expand the words in 1:10, "to wait for His Son from heaven, whom He raised from the dead." In other words, "to wait for His Son from heaven" is to wait for the rapture described in 4:13–18. The rapture is how Jesus "rescues us from the coming wrath" (1:10).

What is the "coming wrath"? Many mistakenly think that the coming wrath in 1 Thessalonians 1:10 means the final, eternal judgment of individuals at the great white throne (Revelation 20:11–15). Instead, we must see that Paul's overview of 1 Thessalonians in 1:9–10 is expanded in 5:1–11. There it is clear that the coming wrath is the tribulation or Seventieth Week of Daniel. In

1 Thessalonians 5:1, Paul begins a slight change of subject from the rapture in chapter 4 to the tribulation or day of the Lord that will immediately follow the rapture.

This transition is made by the phrase *now concerning.* "Now concerning the times and the seasons, brothers, you have no need to have anything written to you. For you yourselves are fully aware that the day of the Lord will come like a thief in the night" (1 Thessalonians 5:1–2 ESV). The reason the Thessalonians did not need to be taught about the times and seasons related to prophecy is that Paul had already taught them about prophecy when he first led them to Christ as Savior. They were fully aware that the day of the Lord would come like a thief in the night.

Do you recognize in this passage terms we have discussed before: the "day of the Lord" and "like a thief in the night"? Paul is clearly borrowing the thief illustration from Jesus' teachings. We know this because neither the Old Testament nor any extra-biblical Jewish writings use this analogy of the thief in prophecy. So Jesus must be the originator. He used the thief imagery both for the rapture and the sudden coming of the day of the Lord. Both the rapture and the onset of the day of the Lord (the tribulation period) must begin as imminent events with no telltale signs to indicate their arrival. Both are surprise, unannounced events. If the rapture happened several months before the tribulation, then the rapture would be a telltale sign of the coming of the tribulation. They must both occur at basically the same time.

As mentioned before, Jesus likened the coming of the day of the Lord to the days of Noah right before he entered the ark. The Lord described the lives of people in Noah's time as "enjoying banquets and parties and weddings right up to the time Noah entered his boat. People didn't realize what was going to happen until the flood came and swept them all away. That is the way it will be when the Son of Man comes" (Matthew 24:38–39). Jesus' description is almost identical to Paul's teaching in 1 Thessalonians 5:3. "While people are saying, 'There is peace and security,' then sudden destruction will come upon them as labor pains come upon a pregnant woman, and they will not escape" (ESV).

Neither Jesus nor Paul mentions radical evil lifestyles as the atmosphere of the world before the destruction of the day of the Lord comes. There are no gross sins mentioned in these descriptions, even though there certainly were gross sins in the days of Noah and will be in the days before Jesus comes. What we find is secular indifference to God and his intervention on earth. The attitude that peace and security exists may not mean that there will be no wars around the world when the tribulation comes. It means that people will be fully convinced that God will not break into the affairs of the world with judgments from heaven. The unbelievers in Noah's day ignored his warnings of the destruction of the coming flood, so they were swept away when the flood came. Just as Noah and his family were safely lifted up above the floodwaters in the ark when the destruction came, so in the rapture, believers will be lifted up and saved from the destruction to come.

In verse 3, Paul also mentions another image we noted before: "Then sudden destruction will come upon them as labor pains come upon a pregnant woman." The image of labor pains helps us understand that Paul is talking about the future tribulation. Since those who have believed in Christ do not go into the tribulation, Paul encouraged the Thessalonians this way: "But you, brothers, are not in the dark, for this day to overtake you like a thief. For you are all sons of light and sons of the day. We do not belong to the night or the darkness. So then, we must not sleep, like the rest, but we must stay awake and be serious" (1 Thessalonians 5:4–6 HCSB).

Paul said that the day of the Lord would not overtake the believers at Thessalonica like a thief. Paul had just described how the tribulation will bring sudden destruction on people and that "they will not escape" (v. 3). Does Paul now mean that the tribulation *will* overtake Christians, just not "like a thief"? That misses his point. He means that the day of the Lord will in no way overtake (or come on) a believer.

We might say, "The sun does not shine at night like it does in the day." In normal (nonscientific) conversation, we would not take this sentence to mean that the sun *does* shine at night, just not the way it does in the daytime. Instead, we mean that the sun doesn't shine *at all* at night. Paul was saying that believers "do not belong to the night or the darkness" so will not enter the tribulation period and its sudden destruction. They will be delivered from God's judgment on earth.

Since like Noah, Christians have this wonderful promise of exemption from the coming divine destructions on earth, we are commanded to "not sleep, like the rest [the unbelievers], but we must stay awake" (v. 6). Paul cannot mean we must stay awake physically. He is speaking of spiritual alertness, spiritual readiness. His challenge calls us to live a godly lifestyle in faith and to be consciously prepared for Jesus' coming in the rapture. We must not be casual about Jesus' return for his followers. Why? "For God did not appoint us to wrath, but to obtain salvation through our Lord Jesus Christ, who died for us, so that whether we are awake or asleep, we will live together with Him. Therefore encourage one another and build each other up as you are already doing" (1 Thessalonians 5:9–11 HCSB).

Through Paul's teaching, we as believers know that "God did not appoint us to wrath." In other words, God sovereignly purposed that all believers since Pentecost should be kept from the judgments of the day of the Lord. Those judgments are intended for unbelievers. Christians are destined to obtain salvation. *Salvation* here means deliverance from the future tribulation by means of the rapture (when we will be resurrected). As believers, "He has died for us, so that whether we are awake [spiritually prepared for the rapture] or asleep [spiritual unprepared], we will live together with Him."

Sometimes in the New Testament, the word *salvation* is used for what we receive at our first act of faith in Christ. This experience is a deliverance from the eternal penalty for our sins. Other times, the word *salvation* is used of our physical resurrection at the rapture (1 Thessalonians 5:10). At this resurrection we are delivered from our sinful nature that resides in our earthly bodies. Paul used the word *salvation* with this second meaning when he said to the believers in the city of Rome, "This [love for others] is all the more urgent, for you know how late it is; time is running out. Wake up, for our salvation [our rapture/resurrection] is nearer now than when we first believed" (Romans 13:11).

Jesus' Teaching About the Rapture in John 14

Two days after Jesus gave his Olivet Discourse, on the night before he was crucified, he talked privately with his disciples in an upstairs room he had selected for the occasion. Judas had left, and Jesus had just predicted that Peter would deny his relationship with Christ three times (John 13:38). (All the other disciples eventually vowed they would never deny Jesus, according to Mark 14:31.) The very next words Jesus said to his disciples were intended for Peter as well.

> Do not let your hearts be troubled. You believe in God; believe also in me. My Father's house has many rooms; if that were not so, would I have told you that I am going there to prepare a place for you? And if I go and prepare a place for you, I will come back and take you to be with me that you also may be where I am.
>
> John 14:1–3 NIV

Jesus prophesied that Peter would deny his relationship to the Lord. Then he told Peter and the others, "Your heart must not despair. I'm going away. But I promise I will come back to take you to be with me forever where I am. I have a special place for you to live with me in my Father's house in heaven." Peter would not lose his salvation, despite his serious sin of denial. Jesus actually assured him of that fact.

At least four of the disciples heard Jesus' Olivet Discourse on Tuesday of that week. They must have remembered that Jesus told them, "Two men will be working together in the field; one will be *taken*, the other left. Two women will be grinding flour at the mill; one will be *taken*, the other left" (Matthew 24:40–41). Jesus was teaching about how he will take someone in the rapture to be with him forever. Now on Thursday, just two days after his Olivet Discourse, Jesus used this same word for "take" when he told the disciples in the upper room, "I will come back and *take* you to be with me." This is the rapture.

Jesus promised to return one day and take us personally, accompanying us back to the Father's house in heaven. He wants us to be with him forever—a deep expression of his love for us.

John's Teaching About the Rapture in Revelation 3:10

There are seven letters in Revelation 2–3 addressed to seven different church congregations in Asia Minor (eastern Turkey today). In these letters, Jesus personally addressed the seven churches, one at a time. One of the churches was the church at a city called Philadelphia. The city of Philadelphia, Pennsylvania, derives its name from this city in the Bible because the city's name comes from two Greek words meaning "brotherly love." A magnificent promise for protection from the judgments of the tribulation is found in the message Jesus gave to the Philadelphian church (Revelation 3:7–13). "Because you have obeyed my command to persevere, I will protect you from the great time of testing that will come upon the whole world to test those who belong to this world" (Revelation 3:10).

The "great time of testing" is the day of the Lord or the tribulation. The tribulation will "test those who belong to this world," i.e., the unbelievers. The primary purpose of the day of the Lord is to test unbelievers, not believers. While there will be great persecution of true Christians (those who come to Christ after the rapture) in the tribulation, the major devastations will be widespread divine judgments sent by God onto the earth. God will not send his wrath on his own children. Only those who are unbelievers will enter the seven years of tribulation.

Some Bible teachers think that the method God uses to protect Christians is to keep us from harm as we go through the tribulation. Then, sometime after we have gone through much or all of the tribulation, we will be raptured to complete safety. A simple reading of the book of Revelation demonstrates that there will be a great many martyrs for their Christian faith in the tribulation.

Revelation 3:10 doesn't say, "I will protect you *in* the great time of testing" but "I will protect you *from* the great time of testing." Many other translations of Revelation 3:10 say something like "I will also keep you from the hour of testing that is going to come over the whole world" (HCSB). To be kept from a burning building means I never get into the burning building in the first place. And to be kept from the hour of testing means I will be kept from going into that time period. In other words, I will be kept from going into the tribulation.

How does God keep true Christians from going into the divine wrath of the tribulation? For the people in the church at Philadelphia, death is the means God used to keep them from the hour of testing. For others who are alive when Jesus comes in the rapture to catch us up to be with him, the method will be the rapture itself. The best understanding of Revelation 3:10 is to see it as a promise of the rapture that will take place before the tribulation begins. Just as Jesus promised to keep believers in the church at Philadelphia out of the time of divine wrath on the earth, so by application, this promise extends to all true believers. We will be kept from those divine judgments associated with "the great time of testing that will come upon the whole world to test those who belong to this world."

5

How Can We Understand the Book of Revelation?

Anyone who is moderately knowledgeable about the Bible knows that the book of Revelation, the last book in the Bible, is challenging to understand. Among all the books of the Bible, the book of Revelation has the widest differences of perspective by Bible interpreters. Some teachers, churches, and denominations hold that most or even all of the prophecies of Revelation have been completely fulfilled—either by AD 70 (the destruction of Jerusalem) or at least by the 1500s (the Protestant Reformation). For some of these Christians, only the coming of Christ to the earth in Revelation 19 and some of the visions of the following chapters are future. Still others believe that most of the book contains unfulfilled prophecy, particularly chapter 4 to the end of the book. All groups agree that the seven letters (chapters 2–3) addressed to seven churches in ancient Asia Minor are historical churches of the first century.

There are several reasons for these differences of interpretation. First, the book contains visions of heaven and heavenly realities using many symbols. The Old Testament book of Daniel contains several occasions where Daniel saw heavenly visions. Most of these visions were interpreted so that he could write them down for others to read. Christians differ as to how many of the visions in Daniel and Revelation are to be taken symbolically and how many are to be taken literally. For example, in Revelation 19:11, John implies that Jesus will return to earth riding on a white horse. Will Jesus literally return riding through the air on a white horse from heaven to earth? Or is the white horse symbolic of a military general riding out victoriously to battle? A further question is: Can this be both literal and symbolic of victory and purity?

Guidelines for Understanding the Book of Revelation

I don't think the book of Revelation is as impossible to understand as some imply. Consider Revelation 5:6: "Then I saw a Lamb that looked as if it had been slaughtered." It is universally accepted that the slaughtered lamb is Jesus. Most of our translations capitalize Lamb to help us with this interpretation. The apostle John, who wrote the book of Revelation, also wrote the gospel of John. There the apostle recorded the words of John the Baptist, "Look! The Lamb of God who takes away the sin of the world!" (John 1:29). As the Jewish people slaughtered a perfect lamb as a sacrifice for their sins, so Jesus was killed as a divine sacrifice for our sins. Jesus isn't a literal lamb, but he was literally sacrificed for our sins like a lamb was sacrificed in the Old Testament. Let me offer a few guidelines by which I interpret the book of Revelation.

Principle #1. Much of Revelation is drawn from prophecies or imagery recorded in the Old Testament, just like the image of a sacrificial lamb. Someone has counted 278 verses in Revelation (out of 404) that are a quote from or an allusion to an Old Testament passage. The majority of Old Testament quotes or allusions are drawn from Daniel, Isaiah, and Ezekiel. The more we know the

Old Testament, the better we will be able to understand the book of Revelation. Revelation 13 speaks of a beast with seven heads and ten horns that "looked like a leopard, but it had the feet of a bear and the mouth of a lion" (Revelation 13:2). To understand this vision, we will need to understand the same images described in Daniel 7. To understand "Babylon the Great, Mother of All Prostitutes" (Revelation 17:5), it will help to know the history of Babylon, beginning with the story of the tower of Babel (Genesis 11:1–9).

Principle #2. Keep in mind that Revelation often interprets itself. For example, consider the rest of Revelation 5:6 cited above: "He [the Lamb] had seven horns and seven eyes." What are the horns and eyes of the Lamb? The verse continues, "which represent the sevenfold Spirit of God that is sent out into every part of the earth." In the Old Testament, horns were often a symbol of power and strength. Animals with horns could defend themselves and even kill other animals or people with their horns. Sometimes numbers are symbolic in Revelation. Seven is a number of perfection and completeness. God created the world in seven days, and he saw that it was good (Genesis 1 mentions this *seven* times). The seven horns and seven eyes represent the complete power and complete knowledge of God. The "sevenfold Spirit of God" is the Holy Spirit sent into the world, having complete knowledge of all things.

There are at least twenty-six examples where Revelation interprets its own symbolism. So look carefully for this. Here are a few more.

What are the seven stars in Jesus' right hand (Revelation 1:16)?
[Jesus is speaking] This is the meaning of the mystery of the seven stars you saw in my right hand and the seven gold lampstands: The seven stars are the angels of the seven churches, and the seven lampstands are the seven churches.

Revelation 1:20

Who is the dragon in Revelation 12–13?
This great dragon—the ancient serpent called the devil, or Satan, the one deceiving the whole world—was thrown down to the earth with all his angels.

Revelation 12:9

Principle #3. A third principle of interpreting Revelation is to ask, "What is the most natural, normal way to take this word or sentence?" This is how language works. Jesus (or God the Father) says in Revelation 1:8, "'I am the Alpha and the Omega—the beginning and the end,' says the Lord God." Alpha and Omega are the first and last letters of the ancient (and modern) Greek alphabet. This is like Jesus saying in English, "I am the A and the Z." Does Jesus mean he is literally two letters of the alphabet? That makes no sense. Pressing the language beyond what is normal shows us that a figure of speech must be involved. Jesus is *like* the first and last letters of the alphabet are to all language and communication. This symbol is redefined in the words "the beginning and the end." Both phrases mean the eternality and infiniteness of Jesus. Nothing exists outside of him.

Numbers in the book of Revelation are interesting—most of them are literal. No one doubts that the seven churches in Revelation 2–3 are seven actual first-century churches. Of course, literal numbers can have symbolic meaning too. But some numbers in Revelation are only symbolic. In Revelation 5:6, cited above, we see a symbolic number. Our default version for this book, the New Living Translation, reads, "He [Jesus] had seven horns and seven eyes, which represent the *sevenfold* Spirit of God" (italics added). Other translations read, "He had seven horns and seven eyes, which are the seven spirits of God" (HCSB). The Holman Christian Standard Bible accurately translates what John wrote in the original Greek language. Why does the NLT use the term "sevenfold Spirit of God" instead of "the seven spirits of God"? Because we know from the rest of the Bible that there is only one (Holy) Spirit, not seven spirits (Ephesians 4:4). He is the third person of the Trinity. We cannot naturally take the seven spirits of God as literal unless it refers to something other than the Holy Spirit. So the NLT is helping us apply principle #3.

Let's apply principle #3 in another passage. Revelation 9:1–11 describes a judgment that comes on the unbelieving people of the world in the tribulation. The shaft of the abyss, or bottomless pit, is opened, and the apostle John sees strange, almost deformed, locusts emerge out of the pit and sting people who are on the earth. The sting will be so dreadfully painful that "people will seek death but will not find it. They will long to die, but death will flee from them!" (Revelation 9:6). John describes the locusts quite differently from typical locusts.

> The locusts looked like horses prepared for battle. They had what looked like gold crowns on their heads, and their faces looked like human faces. They had hair like women's hair and teeth like the teeth of a lion. They wore armor made of iron, and their wings roared like an army of chariots rushing into battle. They had tails that stung like scorpions, and for five months they had the power to torment people.
>
> Revelation 9:7–10

Is it possible that these locusts are real, mutant insects transformed by radical environmental pollution? If so, then John is describing the look of their mutations as best he can. It is more likely that he was describing something that *looked like* giant mutant insects. Notice how often he used the word *like*. The verses leading up to this locust invasion state clearly that the locusts come out of the abyss or bottomless pit (Revelation 9:1–2). The abyss is the location of many fallen angels. Fallen angels are demons or evil spirits (Luke 8:31). The abyss is certainly not the ordinary location for locusts. Their appearance is so different from the locusts we know that it is pressing the language too far to call these mutant locusts. Revelation 9:11 says, "Their king is the angel [demon] from the bottomless pit; his name . . . is . . . the Destroyer." Ordinary locusts don't have a demon as their king. Also, demons can assume various material forms, such as the frogs described in Revelation 16:13. So it is best to understand that part of God's judgment in the tribulation will be to unleash demons who hate God and want to harm people created in God's image (Genesis 1:26–27). That is what is pictured in the vision of Revelation 9.

The Outline of the Book of Revelation

Earlier, we learned that some books of the Bible have an outline of their contents in the introduction of the book. We used Paul's first letter to the Thessalonians as an example. Revelation has this outline as well. The outline for the book is found in 1:19. Jesus tells John, "Therefore write what you have seen, what is, and what will take place after this" (HCSB).

"What you have seen" refers to the vision John received of the glorified Christ in chapter 1. Next, John was to write "what is." This refers to the message John passed on to the seven churches addressed in chapters 2–3. These seven churches are literal churches, but also picture symbolically the complete New Testament church. (Remember that literal numbers can have symbolic meaning too.) Finally, John was told to write "what will take place after this," i.e., after the seven churches (and symbolically, the entire New Testament church) is removed from the scene by means of the rapture. This phrase identifies the rest of the book, which involves the prophetic visions of Revelation 4–22.

Some Bible teachers think that the book of Revelation is not really about future events but about heavenly visions that teach practical and ethical truths about the power of Satan's deception and the need for Christians to persevere in persecution. But the book itself claims to be prophetic. Revelation 1:3 states, "God blesses the one who reads the words of this prophecy to the church." At the close of the book, John falls down to worship an angelic figure. He is given the instructions "No, don't worship me. I am a servant of God, just like you and your brothers the prophets" (22:9). The apostle John is considered to be a "brother" to the great prophets of the Old Testament. Seeing practical and ethical lessons in the book is not contrary to seeing the book as describing future events.

As I mentioned, others believe Revelation contains genuine prophecy, but that the majority of the prophecies have already been fulfilled. If we use principle #3 and understand language as normal communication, the prophecies of Revelation do not seem to be fulfilled unless we read them as highly symbolic and not as normal language. The following example is just one of numerous examples that could be listed. In what is called the seventh bowl judgment, an angel poured out his judgment on the earth. "And a great earthquake struck—the worst since people were placed on the earth" (Revelation 16:18).

The worst earthquake in history was one that occurred in Shaanxi, China, on January 23, 1556. About 830 thousand people died, approximately 60 percent of the region's population. It devastated an area of 520 miles and was felt in ninety-seven countries. This earthquake killed three times more people than the next deadliest earthquake on record. With a world population of about 450 million at the beginning of that century, this death toll amounts to less than 2/10 of a percent (.2%) of the earth's population.

Why should this imagery in Revelation be considered symbolic rather than an actual earthquake (the worst of all times)? When God judges the earth, he will have no problem producing an earthquake of such magnitude.

"What You Have Seen, What Is . . ." (Revelation 1:19a)

Using the outline from Revelation 1:19, here is a brief overview of the first two sections of the book. Revelation 1:1 states, "This is a revelation from Jesus Christ, which God gave him to show his servants the events that must soon take place." Most people have heard the word *apocalypse*. In popular culture, this usually means some kind of complete and final destruction of the world, perhaps similar to what happens in the book of Revelation. Our English word is actually the ancient Greek word in the original New Testament for the word *revelation* in the first verse of the book of Revelation.

Revelation continues with the apostle John's description of receiving the contents of the book by divine authority. He mentions his intended audience: the seven churches of Asia (western Turkey today). Finally, he offers praises to the Father, Son, and Holy Spirit, and announces the second coming of Christ to the earth (1:1–8).

John explains he was imprisoned on the island called Patmos because of his Christian faith. Patmos is a small mountainous island about thirty-five miles off the western coast of Turkey. In the remainder of the chapter (1:9–20), John writes of the vision he saw of "someone like the Son of Man" (v. 13). Son of Man is a messianic title of Jesus as is evident in its background in Daniel 7:13. This interpretation uses principle #1 (the Old Testament background). Jesus often used this messianic title from Daniel in relation to his final return to earth (e.g., Matthew 24:27, 30). In fact, in the prophecies of the Olivet Discourse (including all parallel passages), Jesus used the term *Son of Man* fourteen times.

In the vision of Revelation 1, Jesus was standing in the middle of seven gold lampstands (v. 13). The lampstands are said to symbolize the seven churches of Asia Minor (v. 20). This is principle #2 (Revelation sometimes interprets itself). The light of the lampstands symbolizes the testimony of the churches.

In John's vision of the resurrected and glorified Christ, we see many characteristics that symbolize Christ's complete knowledge, judgment, purity, wisdom, or other attributes of his deity. For example, "His head and his hair were white like wool, as white as snow" (v. 14). This suggests purity, wisdom, and longevity (eternality). Here we apply principle #3. To press the language of this vision in such a way that Jesus, now in heaven, really has white hair, or that literally "a sharp two-edged sword came from his mouth" (v. 16) is probably going too far.

Revelation 2–3 is a unit in which the resurrected and glorified Jesus addresses each of the seven churches of Asia. These seven messages from Jesus are essentially first-century letters. Each letter is addressed to the angel of each church. The word *angel* in the original Greek language of the New Testament could mean just that, an angel. Or, on rare occasions, it is used of human messengers. Since angels are so prominent in Revelation, it seems most probable that the word is used of actual angels.

Following the address to the angel of the church in each letter (chapters 2–3), there is a description of Christ. This description is drawn from the description of Christ as he is revealed in the vision of chapter 1. This description is also related to the individual strengths or weaknesses of each church. To the church at the city of Smyrna, Jesus is identified as the one "who was dead but is now alive" (2:8). Believers were being persecuted in this city, and this description of Jesus encourages them to "remain faithful even when facing death" (v. 10).

Next, the historical background of each church is often relevant to the commands or rewards mentioned to these churches. The church at Laodicea was composed of believers who were complacent about living for Christ. Jesus likened their enthusiasm to water. He said, "You are neither hot nor cold. I wish that you were one or the other! . . . You are like lukewarm water" (3:15–16). The water supply for Laodicea was piped from hot springs originating in a city a few miles north. By the time it reached Laodicea, it was lukewarm. Hot or cold water is pleasing for hot tea or iced tea, but who wants to drink lukewarm water?

Finally, at the end of each letter to the churches, Jesus gives a promise to those believers who overcome. Different views exist regarding the identity of the overcomer and what they are promised. For some, (1) the overcomer is a true Christian and those who do not overcome are those who have never come to faith. According to this view, these first-century churches included a mixture of genuine and false Christians in their assemblies. Another interpretation suggests that (2) the churches are composed of true Christians. But those who become faithless or disobedient lose their salvation. To be an overcomer is to hold on to one's faith and finally enter heaven.

A third view is that (3) the overcomer is a faithful Christian and is rewarded for his or her faithfulness. This is how I understand the promises to the overcomer. The warnings are about the loss of future rewards, not the loss of salvation. It is the works of the believer that are evaluated, not their faith that has brought salvation. Five times Jesus says to these seven churches, "I know your works" (ESV, HCSB). We see that the promises focus on who will become leaders with Christ in his eternal reign. An example of this truth is in Revelation 3:21: "Those who are victorious will sit with me on my throne, just as I was victorious and sat with my Father on his throne."

This is similar to how a presidential candidate gathers around him faithful followers for his campaign. If they remain faithful with him all through his candidacy for office and he wins the election, these associates will be selected to his presidential cabinet. They get to help lead the nation. The twenty-four elders of Revelation 2–3 picture the Lord's "presidential cabinet."

"And What Will Take Place After This" (Revelation 1:19b)

Revelation 4–5 describes a heavenly vision of John when he was caught up to the throne room of God. God was sitting on the throne, with the Lamb (the Lord Jesus) standing before the throne. There were twenty-four elders on twenty-four thrones that encircled the throne of God. The elders were dressed in white and had gold crowns on their heads. The white robes, the crowns, and the thrones represent the future rewards promised to the overcomers in the Asian churches (Revelation 2:10; 3:5, 11, 18, 21). These rewards show that the twenty-four elders are distinct from the angels (cf. Revelation 7:11). They are either all Christians or all faithful Christians.

At what time in the future does this scene take place? First, the elders are pictured in heaven before the coming tribulation judgments described in Revelation 6–19. This means that the rapture has already taken place before the judgments of the tribulation are poured out on the earth. This scene in Revelation 4–5 pictures moments in heaven shortly after the rapture. Second, the elders (believers) have already received their future rewards as is evident by the white robes, thrones, and gold crowns they wear. This suggests that the judgment seat of Christ has already taken place in heaven. The judgment seat of Christ is the occasion in which the life of each Christian will be evaluated to determine his or her future rewards based on one's degree of faithfulness. The judgment seat of Christ is not designed to determine one's eternal destiny in heaven or hell. This judgment will be discussed further in chapter 12.

Four living beings are also around the throne. These living creatures look like a lion, a calf, a man, and a flying eagle. Unlike most angels who don't have wings, these creatures have six wings, not two, each with eyes all around the wings (Revelation 4:6–8). They worship God day and night, and the twenty-four elders fall down and worship God as well.

John announced that in his vision he saw a scroll sealed with seven seals on the inside and outside. The scroll was in the hand of the one seated on the throne. The scroll contained the twenty-one judgments that are to be carried out on the earth. At first, no one in heaven or earth was found worthy to break the seals and open the scroll. After heaven is thoroughly searched, the Lamb who stood before the throne was found to be the only one worthy to open the seal judgments.

Revelation 6–16 describes the twenty-one judgments. They fall into three sets of seven. First are the seven seal judgments. These judgments are revealed as the Lamb breaks the seven seals of the scroll one by one. The trumpet judgments follow, in which seven angels announce these judgments by first blowing a trumpet. After some intervening prophecies, the bowl judgments are announced. Seven angels pour out judgments onto the earth from seven gold bowls.

As you read these chapters, you will see that there are interruptions in the unveiling of these judgments. Usually there is a preliminary event described before judgment #1, followed by judgments #1 to #6. An additional story follows judgment #6 and is climaxed by the seventh judgment in each series. The description of the seventh bowl judgment ends at the end of chapter 16 (16:21).

How Are the Twenty-One Judgments Arranged?

There are differences in how Bible interpreters understand the relationship between the seal, trumpet, and bowl judgments. Are they simply sequential: seven seal judgments, followed by seven trumpet judgments, followed by seven bowl judgments? This view understands the seventh seal judgment to contain the seven trumpet judgments, and the seventh trumpet judgment to contain the seven bowl judgments. The view that sees the judgments overlapping points to the fact that the sixth and seventh judgments of each series seem to bring the prophecies right to the second coming of Christ when compared to other Scriptures.

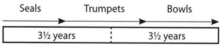

Twenty-One Judgments of Revelation
Sequential View

The overlapping view believes that the three series of judgments contain flashbacks. This is a pattern used elsewhere in the Bible. For example, in Luke 17:24–25, Jesus said, "For as the lightning flashes and lights up the sky . . . so it will be on the day when the Son of Man comes. But first the Son of Man must suffer terribly." In the first sentence (v. 24), Jesus was speaking of his second coming to earth, but then he flashed back to his first coming in the very next verse (v. 25).

Twenty-One Judgments of Revelation
Overlapping View

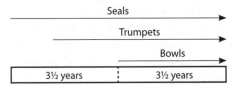

If the overlapping view of the judgments of Revelation is correct, it is designed to hold the reader's attention like flashbacks in a mystery novel. John's desire is to reach a dramatic and suspenseful climax at the end of the twenty-one judgments. He accomplishes this by bringing each set of seven judgments right to the second coming of Christ to the earth, but without actually revealing Christ's return until the end of the story.

Think of the overlapping view like the gradual increase of suspense in a murder mystery on TV. Ten minutes into the program, you are convinced the murderer is the butler. Then a flashback to some past events adds more detail to the story and destroys your theory. Now you are all the more intrigued to identify the murderer. Could it be the secretary? Later a flashback eliminates your theory that the secretary was the culprit. Your curiosity is piqued. At the finale of the movie, a third flashback adds yet more clues. To your utter amazement, the murderer is revealed to be the chauffeur. This technique of flashbacks kept the suspense right to the end of the mystery.

In Revelation 6:2, the first of all the judgments, an unidentified rider on a white horse rides out to conquer. Many interpreters believe that this mystery rider is the Antichrist released at the beginning of the tribulation to begin his conquest of the world. Yet the color white is regularly a symbol of purity and righteousness. In fact, Jesus is clearly identified as a rider on a white horse in Revelation 19 at his coming to earth (v. 11).

In my understanding, the first judgment in Revelation is Jesus as a mystery rider on a white horse going forth to conquer the world and rule over it. At the climax of the book, Jesus also rides a white horse to conquer his enemies and rule the world. Jesus begins and ends the judgments of the tribulation in Revelation.

From the world's perspective, this mystery rider and the source of the earth's catastrophes are hidden until the very end of the tribulation. Then the people clearly see that these disasters are judgments coming from heaven. The rider in Revelation 6 initiates this great victory; the rider in Revelation 19 completes this great victory. Through a series of flashbacks that maintain the suspense of the reader, the book of Revelation keeps the full disclosure of the mysterious, conquering rider on the white horse until the climax of the story.

Similarities Between Trumpet and Bowl Judgments

1. Earth
2. Sea
3. Freshwaters
4. Heavenly Bodies
5. Darkness
6. Euphrates
7. Lightning, Thunder, Earthquakes

Whatever one's view of the chronology of the twenty-one judgments, one thing is certain: There is an increasing intensity of the judgments the further they progress. The final judgments are more severe than the initial judgments. Also, the trumpet judgments are characterized by the fraction one-third. For example, in the first trumpet judgment, "one-third of the earth was set on fire," and "one-third of the trees were burned" (8:7). In the second trumpet judgment, "one-third of the water in the sea became blood, one-third of all things living in the sea died, and one-third of all the ships on the sea were destroyed" (8:8–9).

There are also some similarities between the trumpet judgments and the bowl judgments. See the chart for these similarities. These parallels lead to the possibility that after one-third of the earth, sea, or freshwaters, etc., are affected in the seven trumpet judgments, they may recover for a short time only to have the bowl judgments destroy them again.

After the twenty-one judgments are revealed, another anti-climactic event takes place in the story. Revelation 17–18 details the nature and final destruction of a prostitute that rides a seven-headed beast. The prostitute is clearly symbolic because she is identified as the city of Babylon (17:18). This woman (or city) is said to have "committed sexual immorality" with all the kings of the earth. Chapters 17–18 are dedicated to describing Babylon's radical destruction. Revelation 19 carries on the theme of the city's destruction with four announcements of Hallelujah and praises to God because the city was forever destroyed (19:1–6).

The wedding of the Lamb to his bride (believers in the church age) and the wedding banquet are also announced in Revelation 19. The remainder of the chapter describes Jesus' return to earth and the following warfare between the nations of the earth and Christ. More details on this battle will be given in chapters 9 and 10, "What Is Armageddon?" and "What Is the Second Coming of Christ to the Earth?" In short, Christ will overwhelmingly defeat all his enemies who are attempting to keep him from ruling over the earth.

Once Christ has defeated his enemies, he will set up his rule over the earth (Revelation 20). First, Satan will be confined for the one-thousand-year rule of Jesus over the earth. Those who were martyred in the tribulation will be resurrected and become rulers in Jesus' kingdom. This worldwide rule will be accompanied by peace until the very end of the one thousand years. At that time, Satan will be released for a short time and will lead an unsuccessful, final rebellion on earth. After Christ's victory, the great white throne judgment will take place. This judgment is for all those who, throughout all history, have rejected faith in the one true God of Israel (Old Testament era) or faith in Jesus Christ (New Testament era).

God will not abandon his original design for the world. He will instead remake the old earth and the old heavens into a new heaven and earth (Revelation 21). Its central city will be the New

Jerusalem. This new world will never experience the sin that overpowered the old heavens and old earth. God will come down and live with people on the new earth for all eternity (Revelation 21–22). The final words of Revelation stress the certainty of Christ's return and warn sternly against those who would try to add or distort the truth contained in the book.

6

Who Is the Antichrist?

It is actually startling to discover how many really evil people have come and gone in human history. Most of us can think of a few by name from recent times. Perhaps we think of Adolf Hitler, the dictator of Germany from 1933 to his death in 1945. Hitler was directly responsible for the deaths of 11 million people, including more than 1 million children and 6 million Jews. His medical experimentations not only killed thousands, they also permanently maimed hundreds of thousands. Joseph Stalin was the brutal dictator of the Soviet Union from 1922 to 1953. It is estimated that Stalin killed somewhere between 20 to 60 million people. More recently we can think of various Islamic terrorists or leaders such as Saddam Hussein (president of Iraq, 1979–2003), one of the most brutal tyrants in recent history, and Osama bin Laden (1957–2011), who claimed responsibility for the 9/11 (2001) attacks against the United States that killed nearly three thousand people.

Similar atrocities were carried out by rulers in the distant past. Caligula was Rome's third emperor (AD 37–41). He brutally murdered people just for entertainment. He killed most of his own family and most of his important friends. Nero was the Roman Empire's fifth emperor (AD 54–68). He burned the city of Rome, killing many of his own citizens and leaving hundreds of thousands destitute. He also murdered most of his own family and relatives. He tortured and killed numerous Christians, including both Paul and Peter, the most well-known apostles of the early Christian church. Many of the inhumane brutalities, tortures, rapes, and abominable lifestyles of these rulers are best left unmentioned. None of these evil rulers compare to the one the Bible describes as the Antichrist, a future wicked world ruler. The Bible says, "He [will be] given authority to rule over every tribe and people and language and nation" (Revelation 13:7).

The Antichrist will be both a political and religious figure. The term *antichrist* has an apparent double meaning in the Bible. The word *anti* used in the original Greek language of the New Testament primarily means "against." The English prefix *anti-* on words such as anti-inflammatory or antifreeze has this meaning. In this sense, the Antichrist will be against Jesus, in radical opposition to the true Christ or true Messiah. *Anti* in ancient Greek also means "in place of, instead of." This meaning may suggest that the Antichrist will claim deceitfully to be the real Christ, or at least the Savior of the world, when he is not.

The name *Antichrist* only shows up in two small books of the New Testament, in 1 and 2 John, and is used only four times. The apostle John (the same apostle who wrote the book of Revelation) wrote to his followers, "Dear children [a common term used for one's disciples in the early Christian culture], the last hour is here. You have heard that the Antichrist is coming, and already many such antichrists have appeared. From this we know that the last hour has come" (1 John 2:18). Notice that John's readers had already "heard that the Antichrist is coming." They were taught prophecy. They were also warned about "many antichrists" that were already in the world. These are false leaders and false teachers who deny that Jesus is the Messiah (or the Christ) (2:22).

By the "last hour," John pictures the whole time from the death and resurrection of Jesus to his final return to earth. Earlier I mentioned that the term *last days* sometimes has this meaning. John also wrote that anyone who teaches that Jesus is not the Christ (or Messiah) is definitely not from God. "Such a person has the spirit of the Antichrist, which you heard is coming into the world and indeed is already here" (4:3).

While the spirit of antichrist is already working in those who teach false ideas about the Bible and Jesus, the Antichrist himself is still future. Satan is a spirit being, a fallen angel. The Antichrist will be his human instrument much like Satan used Judas Iscariot to betray Jesus and bring about Jesus' crucifixion. In other words, Satan will control this wicked person, the Antichrist, who is yet to be revealed to the world. Revelation pictures Satan symbolically as a dragon and the Antichrist as a beast. "And the dragon gave the beast his own power and throne and great authority" (Revelation 13:2). The Antichrist will rise to a prominent political position that will eventually lead to his dictatorship of the entire world. Just as Germany submitted to Hitler, or Rome yielded to Nero's rule, the apostle John declared in his vision of the future that "the whole world . . . gave allegiance to the beast" (v. 3).

The Antichrist has several other names in the Bible. As is evident in the Bible verses above, Revelation often calls him "the beast." Revelation refers to a beast that symbolizes a *collection of nations*—a composite beast—opposed to Israel and to New Testament Christians. But some passages in Revelation refer to the beast as a *future person* who emerges from one of these nations. I will usually refer to this evil person as the Antichrist. When I capitalize the word *Beast*, I will be speaking of the same individual.

As we have noted before, some Christians believe that most of the book of Revelation was already fulfilled in the first century. They understand that the Beast of Revelation 13 is not a future world ruler. Instead, they believe the verses about the Beast have been fulfilled by a Roman emperor such as Nero. As we will see later, the books of Daniel and Revelation predict that the Antichrist will desecrate the rebuilt temple in Jerusalem in an event that the Bible calls "the abomination that causes desolation." An image or statue of the Beast will be set up in the rebuilt Jerusalem temple, and the whole world will be required to worship him or be put to death (Revelation 13:14–17). Nero never actually visited Jerusalem or its temple, so he could not have fulfilled this prophecy.

Will the Antichrist Be a Muslim or a Jew?

Some Bible teachers and preachers understand the Antichrist to be a Jew. They suggest that if the Jewish people will make a covenant with the Antichrist, and they will according to Daniel 9:27, then the Antichrist must be a Jew. Additionally, if *antichrist* means "in place of Christ (or Messiah)," then the Antichrist must be Jewish to replace the true Messiah. The Jews would never accept a Gentile as their true Messiah.

No clear passage suggests that the Antichrist will be Jewish or that the Jews will accept the Antichrist as their Messiah. In the Old Testament, Israel was often threatened with invasion from foreign nations. God promised them protection if they would trust him. Repeatedly, in disobedience, they sought out Gentile nations (e.g., Egypt) for their protection and safety. In the tribulation, they will repeat this spiritual blunder by turning to a Gentile (the Antichrist) and a Gentile nation for protection.

In Daniel 9:26–27, we saw that the Antichrist was from the same people group as the nation that destroyed the temple in AD 70. It was the Romans who destroyed the Jerusalem temple in AD 70. The Romans were Gentiles. This suggests that the Antichrist will be a Gentile. The same is true in Revelation 13, where the Antichrist is called the Beast. The Beast comes up out of the sea. In the Old Testament, the sea is often symbolic of the masses of Gentile people in the world in chaotic rebellion against God.

It will be helpful to understand that Scripture mentions a symbol that sometimes describes a kingdom and at other times describes the ruler of that kingdom. The same symbol is used for both. For example, in the prophecy of Daniel 2, King Nebuchadnezzar had a vision at night in which he saw a huge statue. Daniel interpreted the dream for Nebuchadnezzar. The head of the statue was made of gold. In Daniel 2:38, Daniel told Nebuchadnezzar, "*You* are the head of gold." So Nebuchadnezzar himself was the head of the statue. Then Daniel told the king, "After you, there will arise another *kingdom*, inferior to yours, and then another, a third kingdom" (Daniel 2:39 HCSB). So the head of gold represents the kingdom of Babylon as well as the king of Babylon.

In Revelation, the beast represents an empire structured around a league of Gentile nations (the Roman Empire II of the tribulation period). The king over this empire/league of nations will be the Antichrist. It is unlikely that a Jew would be king over Gentile nations. Even more, 2 Thessalonians 2:4 states that the Antichrist will reject all other gods or objects of worship and demand that the world worship him and him alone. If the Antichrist is Jewish or Muslim, he will turn against his faith and demand worldwide worship. All Jews and all Muslims will need to convert to Antichrist worship or die.

Finally, if the Antichrist is a Muslim, it is difficult to believe that the Jewish people will sign an agreement with him to protect them from other nations as Daniel 9 implies. Will Israeli leaders turn to a committed Islamic ruler when the Qur'an teaches its followers to annihilate the Jews?

How Will People Identify the Antichrist?

There are other names given in the Bible for the Antichrist. In the apostle Paul's second letter to the Thessalonians, he describes the Antichrist's true character as the "man of lawlessness." The Thessalonians had received some kind of counterfeit communication that was supposedly from Paul. Apparently, it had said or implied that the rapture had taken place and the tribulation had begun. The Thessalonians were upset—and no wonder. Had they missed the rapture? Were they in the tribulation? Paul calmed their fears and gave them an explanation as to how they might determine when the tribulation was under way. If they could not see these evidences, then they would know that they were not in the tribulation period.

Don't be fooled by what they say. For that day [the day of the Lord] will not come until there is a great rebellion against God and the man of lawlessness is revealed—the one who brings destruction. He will exalt himself and defy everything that people call god and every object of worship. He will even sit in the temple of God, claiming that he himself is God. . . . He can be revealed only when his time comes. . . . Then the man of lawlessness will be revealed, but the Lord Jesus will kill him with the breath of his mouth and destroy him by the splendor of his coming. This man will come to do the work of Satan with counterfeit power and signs and miracles. He will use every kind of evil deception to fool those on their way to destruction, because they refuse to love and accept the truth that would save them.

2 Thessalonians 2:3–4, 6, 8–10

It isn't hard to believe that "a great rebellion against God" will occur right after the rapture as the tribulation begins. For immediately at the onset of the tribulation, everyone in the world will be one who has never placed his or her faith in Jesus as Savior. Most of the genuinely kind and loving people in the world (those who believe in Jesus) will have disappeared from the earth. Of course, many people will believe in Jesus for the first time as the tribulation proceeds.

In these verses, Paul explains to the Thessalonians that if they don't see this "great rebellion against God" and if they don't see the "man of lawlessness" clearly revealed to the world, they can be assured that the tribulation has not begun and they have not missed the rapture.

Very early in the tribulation, a world leader will emerge who will sign a treaty with Israel to protect that nation (Daniel 9:27). In addition, people should recognize quickly, as Paul said, that "counterfeit power and signs and miracles" will accompany the Antichrist's rise to prominence. This will help identify him as the Antichrist. After three and a half years, he will break this peace treaty. Keep this in mind: No one will be able to positively identify the Antichrist until after the rapture and the tribulation is under way. While he may be alive in the world today, he will not be revealed as the Antichrist until after the tribulation begins.

Who Is the "False Prophet"?

The Antichrist will have an evil accomplice to promote his rise to power. He is called the False Prophet in three different verses in Revelation. Revelation 19:20 says, "And the beast [the Antichrist] was captured, and with him the false prophet who did mighty miracles on behalf of the beast—miracles that deceived all who had accepted the mark of the beast and who worshiped his statue." John also called the False Prophet a beast. John wrote, "I saw another beast come up out of the earth. He had two horns like those of a lamb, but he spoke with the voice of a dragon" (Revelation 13:11). The Beast came up "out of the earth." This could be translated "out of the *land*," meaning out of the land of Israel. If this is correct, then the False Prophet would be Jewish. The Old Testament often warned of false prophets in Israel. The fact that the False Prophet had "two horns like those of a lamb" could also imply that he was Jewish. Jesus warned his early Jewish followers, "Beware of false prophets who come disguised as harmless sheep" (Matthew 7:15).

The False Prophet will command everyone everywhere to worship the Antichrist. In John's vision, he saw the False Prophet performing "astounding miracles, even making fire flash down to earth from the sky while everyone was watching. And with all the miracles he was allowed to perform on behalf of the first beast [the Antichrist], he deceived all the people who belong to this world" (Revelation 13:13–14).

The Death and Resurrection of the Antichrist

Satan is not very original. His creative powers merely imitate God's creative powers. We find in Revelation 12–13 a satanic trinity that imitates the divine Trinity: the Father, the Son, and the Holy Spirit. In the book of Revelation, Satan acts like God the Father, the Antichrist acts like Jesus, and the False Prophet acts like the Holy Spirit.

What would make the whole world decide to worship the Antichrist? For one thing, he will appear to come back to life from a fatal wound, probably suffered in military warfare. In other words, the Antichrist will attempt to replace Jesus by imitating a death and resurrection. In his vision, John said the Antichrist (one of the heads of the composite beast) "appeared to be fatally wounded, but his fatal wound was healed. The whole earth was amazed and followed the beast. They worshiped the dragon [Satan] because he gave authority to the beast. And they worshiped the beast, saying, 'Who is like the beast? Who is able to wage war against him?'" (Revelation 13:3–4 HCSB).

Satan doesn't have the innate power to raise anyone from the dead. On the other hand, no one would be amazed or worship the Antichrist if his death were a fake. Later in Revelation 13, the Antichrist is said to be the one "who was fatally wounded and then came back to life" (v. 14). This language doesn't sound like his death was only a counterfeit or a hoax.

The answer may be that God will, this one time, give Satan the miraculous power to resurrect the Antichrist. Just as people worship Jesus because of his death and resurrection, so those in the tribulation who refuse to believe in Jesus for eternal life will worship the Beast instead because he dies and comes back to life again. In this case, the "anti-" in Antichrist carries the sense "instead of, in place of." The Antichrist will attempt to replace Christ.

The Abomination That Causes Desolation

The phrase *abomination of desolation* is a term that has been used for many years in many versions of the Bible (ESV, NKJV, NASB). More recently, modern versions have tried to clarify this mysterious term by translating, "the abomination that causes desolation" (HCSB, NIV), "the sacrilegious object that causes desecration" (NLT), "the desolating sacrilege" (NRSV), "the appalling abomination" (NJB), or a similar phrase. I will use the term *the abomination that causes desolation*.

Jesus, in his Olivet Discourse, instructed his disciples, "So when you see the abomination that causes desolation, spoken of by the prophet Daniel, standing in the holy place . . . then those in Judea must flee to the mountains!" (Matthew 24:15–16 HCSB). Mark 13 is a parallel passage where the Olivet Discourse is also recorded. Mark 13:14 is the precise parallel to Matthew 24:15. An insight is found in the original Greek language of these verses. Matthew 24 implies that the abomination is an object (e.g., a statue); Mark 13 implies that the abomination is a male person. At first, this seems like a contradiction. As the abomination that causes desolation is given added details in the book of Revelation, it becomes evident that both are true.

Just as Jesus said, this abomination was mentioned directly by Daniel. Daniel prophesied in chapter 9 that after sixty-nine weeks (483 years), the Messiah would be "cut off and will have nothing." Then, after an intervening gap of time, the Antichrist "will make a firm covenant with many for one week [seven years], but in the middle of the week he will put a stop to sacrifice and offering. And the abomination of desolation will be on a wing of the temple [for the last three and a half years] until the decreed destruction is poured out on the desolator" (9:26–27 HCSB).

From this verse we can conclude that the abomination that causes desolation is a sacrilege that will take place in the Jerusalem temple, but not until the very middle of the tribulation. Part of the sacrilege will be that the Antichrist "will put a stop to sacrifice and offering" in the temple. This is clear evidence that the Jewish temple must be rebuilt in Jerusalem, and have priests offering genuine sacrifices, at least by the middle of the tribulation.

As we pointed out above, according to Jesus, "when you see the abomination that causes desolation, spoken of by the prophet Daniel, standing in the holy place . . . then those in Judea must flee to the mountains!" (Matthew 24:15–16 HCSB). What will the Jewish people in Israel see? Second Thessalonians 2:4 says that the Antichrist "will exalt himself and defy everything that people call god and every object of worship. He will even sit in the temple of God, claiming that he himself is God." First, they will see the Antichrist enthrone himself in the rebuilt Jerusalem temple, proclaiming that he is the one true God. But he will not stay in the temple for days and months. He will have many other places to go in order to carry out his domination of the world.

In his absence, what will continue to desecrate the temple? And what is it that people will see that will cause the desolation? What will cause the temple to be barren and desolate of all true believers in the God of the Bible?

> He [the False Prophet] ordered the people to make a great statue of the first beast [the Antichrist], who was fatally wounded and then came back to life. He was then permitted to give life to this statue so that it could speak. Then the statue of the beast commanded that anyone refusing to worship it must die.
>
> Revelation 13:14–15

The False Prophet will instigate the construction of a statue in the image of the Antichrist. This idol will be placed in the temple and will carry on the abomination Daniel described. The fact that the False Prophet is able "to give life to this statue so that it could speak" implies a satanic miracle, not computer animations, human trickery, or magic.

Anyone who worships the Beast or his statue in the Jerusalem temple will automatically consign themselves to eternal damnation and the punishment of the lake of fire. This includes those who receive the mark of the Beast as well. "Then a third angel followed them, shouting, 'Anyone who worships the beast and his statue or who accepts his mark on the forehead or on the hand . . . will be tormented with fire and burning sulfur in the presence of the holy angels and the Lamb'" (Revelation 14:9–10).

What Is the Mark of the Beast?

Years ago, a Christian woman called me on the phone, extremely upset because she thought she had received the mark of the Beast. For a business party, her employer had stamped her hand with an invisible mark, the kind that is visible only under an ultraviolet light. She was concerned that she had secretly received the mark of the Beast as taught in the book of Revelation. I repeatedly assured her that absolutely no one will ever receive the mark of the Beast without consciously knowing what they are doing. That is because, according to the book of Revelation, everyone who receives the mark of the Beast will consciously and willingly worship the Antichrist and his image constructed in the rebuilt temple in Jerusalem.

Besides that, no one will be able to buy or sell anything if they do not receive the mark of the Beast. Revelation 13:16–17 states, "He [the False Prophet] required everyone—small and great, rich and poor, free and slave—to be given a mark on the right hand or on the forehead. And no one could buy or sell anything without that mark, which was either the name of the beast or the number representing his name." Even a garage sale will be forbidden without the mark of the Beast. No distinctions are made between the upper class and lower class. No area of the world will be exempt, with the possible exception of isolated tribal cultures. Regardless, there will be many who come to faith and refuse to take the mark of the Beast. Most of them will be beheaded for their faith, and receive special honor with Christ in the future kingdom of one thousand years (Revelation 20:4).

Many people wonder what type of mark will be used by the Antichrist. Scripture doesn't make this clear. The ancient world, including the Roman Empire, did use marks and religious tattoos to identify a devotee to a particular god. They were visible marks, of course. Revelation 13:18 suggests a number might be the mark itself. "Wisdom is needed here. Let the one with understanding solve the meaning of the number of the beast, for it is the number of a man. His number is 666."

In some ancient languages, such as Hebrew and Greek, the letters of the alphabet also had numerical equivalents. The letters of any person's name could be added to determine a total value. The first ten letters would equal the numbers 1–10. The next ten letters were numbers 20, 30, etc., up to 100. The following letters were increments of 100, and so on. Every person's name had a numerical value. Many attempts have been made in the past and in the present to identify the number (mark) of the Antichrist.

The identification of the Antichrist or his mark is futile until the tribulation begins. One important point of Revelation 13:18 is that the number of the Beast, 666, is "the number of a man [of a human being]." God created humans on the sixth day of creation. The number six probably symbolizes what is finite or human. Three is the number of perfection in the Bible. Three sixes represent a man's attempt to reach perfection, to be the Trinity, the three persons who are one God. The number six falls short of God's perfection, and three sixes fall short of the triune God.

Man is only a created being, radically inferior to the creator God. Wisdom requires that those who believe in Christ see that the Antichrist is no more than a finite, human being despite his worldwide power. He will be totally destroyed by a single word from the mouth of Jesus at the second coming of Christ to the earth. The Antichrist is just a puny human being compared with Jesus—nothing more.

The Final Judgment of the Antichrist and the False Prophet

The final judgment of the Antichrist and the False Prophet is both sudden and complete. In 2 Thessalonians 2:8, Paul said, "The Lord Jesus will destroy him [the man of lawlessness] with the breath of His mouth and will bring him to nothing with the brightness of His coming" (HCSB). Revelation 19:20 states that at Christ's coming to earth, "the beast was captured, and with him the false prophet who did mighty miracles on behalf of the beast—miracles that deceived all who had accepted the mark of the beast and who worshiped his statue. Both the beast and his false prophet were thrown alive into the fiery lake of burning sulfur."

Have you ever seen a film clip of crowds and crowds of people lifting their right arms and saluting as they cry, "Heil Hitler! Heil Hitler!"? Magnify that picture multiple times in your mind. Imagine it as a worldwide phenomenon. That's a picture of the formidable deception that will sweep over the planet as people worship the Antichrist.

7

What Is the Role of Israel in the End Times?

Once the King of Prussia, Frederick II (1740–1786), questioned one of his generals, who often told him about Christ and the king's need for faith in him as Savior. Frederick frequently replied in jest and questioned the existence of God. One day the king challenged the general's insistence that the Bible was God's special revelation. "Give me a proof for the truth of the Bible in just two words." The general replied, "Your majesty, the Jews." The general was referring to the phenomenal preservation of the Jews as a people and a nation as prophesied in the Bible.

Consider some of these facts. The Jewish people are the only ethnicity that has remained a distinct people group after being exiled to more than seventy different countries over a span of twenty centuries. In the Bible alone, we read that the Jews were deported to Assyria, Babylonia, Persia, Greece, and Rome. The Jews continued to be dispersed from their land under the Roman emperor Hadrian (AD 135), were severely persecuted during the Byzantine era (AD fourth to sixth centuries), and were invaded by Muslims in the seventh century. In modern times, the Holocaust of World War II killed 6 million Jews in an attempt to annihilate their race. Besides their own preservation, the Jews are the only people group that has successfully revived their ancient Hebrew language (begun in the late 1800s) after more than two thousand years. Most ancient nations spoke languages that are now dead, like Latin or Egyptian.

The Jews are a special people group chosen by God. In their history, God certainly punished Israel for their sin. But he would not and will not eliminate them as a people or a nation. The prophet Jeremiah said, "'I am with you and will save you,' declares the LORD. 'Though I completely destroy all the nations among which I scatter you, I will not completely destroy you'" (30:11 NIV). A little later in his writings, Jeremiah also prophesied about Israel, "The LORD has made a promise to Israel. . . . The LORD affirms, 'The descendants of Israel will not cease forever to be a nation in my sight. That could only happen if the fixed ordering of the heavenly lights were to cease to operate before me'" (31:35–36 NET).

From 605 BC, when the Jewish nation was first conquered by the Babylonians (modern Iraq), until 1948, Israel was not in control of its own land. During the lifetime of Jesus, the Romans were in governmental control of the land. In modern times, the Jewish people began to immigrate back to their land of Israel in 1881. It was actually as a result of the suffering of the Jewish people during the Holocaust of World War II that the nation was granted its own land and its independence once again. From 605 BC until 1948, Israel was not a self-governed nation. This is an amazing fulfillment of prophecy.

Apart from those who take the Bible seriously, who would have suggested seventy-five years ago that the world's greatest issues would eventually be focused on a tiny portion of the Middle East?

Has God Permanently Cast Israel Aside?

Some Christians think that God has permanently set aside Israel as a nation. This is a mistake. God doesn't abolish his promises so quickly, nor does he take defeat lightly. He didn't allow sin to dominate his plans for people. When death entered the human race, God found a way to defeat it. Jesus died to both forgive and defeat sin. He didn't abandon his design of the human body either. He will redeem the physical body through resurrection. He did not abandon his plans for the heavens and the earth. He will remake them into the new heaven and the new earth. God will also keep his promises to Israel. He will again work with that nation, bringing them to faith in his Son, Jesus.

The apostle Paul wrote to the Christians in Rome, "I ask, then, has God rejected his own people, the nation of Israel? Of course not! . . . No, God has not rejected his own people, whom he chose from the very beginning" (Romans 11:1–2). Paul explained that now was God's time of turning to the Gentiles. One reason God did this was so that the Gentiles might provoke Jewish people to faith. "Did God's people stumble and fall beyond recovery? Of course not! They were disobedient, so God made salvation available to the Gentiles. But he wanted his own people [the Jews] to become jealous and claim it for themselves" (11:11). What did God really want by bringing Gentiles to faith? Read the last sentence of that verse again. God's purpose in bringing salvation to the Gentiles was ultimately designed for his Jewish people.

Paul compared the promises made to Abraham to the root of an olive tree. He likened believing Jewish people to a natural branch on the olive tree, but the believing Gentiles he likened to a wild branch grafted into the tree. In this present age, wild olive branches have been grafted into the olive tree and receive life from its root. Therefore, Gentiles receive the blessings of salvation spoken to Abraham. Paul warned the Gentiles not to be arrogant against the Jews. The Gentiles needed to keep in mind that they were the wild branches grafted into the olive tree, not the natural branches.

Most Christians think it's harder for God to cultivate faith in Jesus among Jewish people than it is to cultivate the same faith among Gentile people. This is not exactly Paul's perspective. The Jews were the natural branches. As the natural branches, it will be easier for God to bring the Jewish people back to faith in their Messiah. "You Gentiles are like the branch of a wild olive tree that is broken off and then, contrary to nature, is joined to a cultivated olive tree. The Jews are like this cultivated tree; and *it will be much easier for God* to join these broken-off branches to their own tree again" (Romans 11:24 TEV).

In the end times, God will work with Israel again. He will graft back into the cultivated tree the natural branches (the Jewish people). Paul said, "And so all Israel will be saved" (Romans 11:26). In other words, during the final days of the tribulation, a majority, if not all, of the Jewish people living will come to faith in Jesus as their Messiah.

The Jewish People and the Tribulation

The Time for Israel. Earlier we learned that Daniel 9:24–27 predicted a future seven-year period. This period was designed primarily for the Jewish people, not the people of the New Testament church. Daniel 9:24 began the prophecy, "A period of seventy sets of seven has been decreed for your people." "Your people" means Daniel's people, the Jews. So the seven-year tribulation is first and foremost a time for the Jewish people, not for believers of the church. That's one reason believers in the age of the church are not called to go through the tribulation. It isn't designed for them.

The Treaty with Israel. Daniel 9:24–27 also describes a treaty with Israel made by the Antichrist. Daniel 9:27 says, "And he [the Antichrist] shall make a strong covenant with many [in Jewish leadership] for one week [seven years], and for half of the week [three and a half years] he shall put an end to sacrifice and offering" (ESV). This time for Israel and this treaty with Israel also means trouble for Israel. Earlier we cited Jeremiah 30:7, showing that the day of the Lord, or tribulation, was called a "time of distress for Jacob" (ESV).

The Trouble for Israel. Another picture of the trouble for Israel is found in the vision John had in Revelation 12. John "saw

94

a woman clothed with the sun, with the moon beneath her feet, and a crown of twelve stars on her head" (v. 1). This woman was pregnant, and "cried out because of her labor pains and the agony of giving birth" (v. 2). Once again, the Old Testament background is essential for understanding the vision. Genesis 37:9–10 makes it clear that the woman represents Israel corporately and the twelve stars are the twelve tribes of Israel. Mary, the mother of Jesus, is also a part of Israel. So the vision pictures Israel and Mary (a corporate group and an individual) about to give birth to their Messiah. Once again, the reference to "labor pains" of a pregnant woman pictures the struggles of Israel at the first coming of Christ as well as their troubles at the second coming of Christ.

John also saw a large red dragon (Satan) who "stood in front of the woman as she was about to give birth, ready to devour her baby as soon as it was born" (Revelation 12:4). This scene depicts how Satan used Herod the Great (47–4 BC). He was king over Judea at the birth of Jesus and killed all the male babies in Bethlehem two years old and under. This was an attempt to kill the baby Jesus who was prophesied to be a king (Matthew 2:1–3, 16).

Herod was right. Jesus will be king. But neither Herod nor Satan can defeat God. "She gave birth to a son who was to rule all nations with an iron rod" (Revelation 12:5). Here we find the principle of telescoping again. "She gave birth to a son" is the first coming of Christ. Jesus will also "rule all nations with an iron rod." This is the second coming of Christ. More than two thousand years has intervened between the first and last part of this verse.

The Rapture in Revelation 12

People in the Western world think individually. It is difficult for us to think corporately. We make individual decisions despite what our parents say or what our friends would choose. Outside of the Western world, people often think and decide in groups. In some cultures, a son must never make a decision apart from the advice of his father and grandfather. When I suggest that the "woman" in the vision of John represents both Israel (a group) and Mary (an individual Jew within Israel), this might be strange or difficult for some to comprehend.

Since I am discussing Revelation 12:5, let me add a further thought not directly related to Israel's future but important to prophecy. In Revelation 12:5, the son is also an individual and a corporate idea or group. This is an even more difficult idea for us to grasp. The son to whom the woman gives birth is certainly Jesus, the Messiah. But the "son" is also united with all true Christian believers in this vision. When people receive Jesus as their Savior, they are united to Jesus in a special spiritual but invisible unity. They are also joined spiritually and invisibly with every other true Christian.

The Bible calls this union of all believers with Jesus "the body of Christ." Paul said, "He [Jesus] is the Savior of his body, the church" (Ephesians 5:23). This is the invisible church, not the visible buildings where Christians gather. In another passage, Paul taught, "All of you together [who believe in Jesus] are Christ's body, and each of you is a part of it" (1 Corinthians 12:27). The son in this vision in Revelation 12 is first of all Jesus. Secondarily, the son (Jesus) includes his entire body (i.e., the body of Christ), the invisible church.

Here is the fascinating part of the prophecy. The apostle John tells us that the woman's "child was snatched away from the dragon and was caught up to God and to his throne." The words *snatched away* and *caught up* are just one Greek word. Our first thought is that *caught up* refers to the ascension of Christ forty days after his resurrection. But in the New Testament, this Greek word for *caught up* is never used of the ascension of Christ.

It is the same Greek word in 1 Thessalonians 4:17 that Paul used to describe the rapture of the church, Christ's body. In Revelation 12:5, Christ's body corporately, the church, is caught up to heaven. That's the corporate aspect of the Son. It is Jesus' body, the church, that is caught up or snatched up to God. Satan has always attempted to devour the Son (the church), starting with its very beginning. Just read the book of Acts. One can quickly see behind the scenes that Satan is at work to destroy the church (e.g., Acts 5:3). The Son (the body of Christ) was "snatched away from the dragon" by the rapture. Once the rapture takes place, God focuses on Israel again.

The Jewish People and the Tribulation, Continued

According to Revelation 12, John watched as "the woman [Israel] fled into the wilderness, where God had prepared a place to care for her for 1,260 days" (v. 6). The 1,260 days clearly point to half of the Seventieth Week of Daniel or to three and a half years. These days must be the second half of the seven-year tribulation. This seems evident from Jesus' teachings. We noted earlier that Jesus instructed future Jewish believers when he addressed his own Jewish disciples, telling them, "So when you see the abomination that causes desolation, spoken of by the prophet Daniel, standing in the holy place . . . then those in Judea must flee to the mountains!" (Matthew 24:15–16 HCSB). The abomination that causes desolation will take place at the midpoint of the tribulation. This marks the beginning of serious persecution for Israel. The Jewish believers must flee to the mountains in the desert.

Revelation 12 also tells us that at the middle of the tribulation, Satan will be kicked out of heaven, along with all his demonic cohorts. Satan is a created but fallen being and cannot be everywhere at once like the creator God. What is he doing in heaven? Revelation 12:10 tells us, "The accuser [Satan] of our brothers and sisters has been thrown down to earth—the one who accuses them before our God day and night." The accuser is not his only name in this passage. He is given five other names in 12:9. Count them: "This *great dragon*— the *ancient serpent* called the *devil*, or *Satan*, the *one deceiving the whole world*—was thrown down to the earth with all his angels."

Sometime before the midpoint of the tribulation, there will be an angelic war in heaven. Satan will be kicked out of heaven and barred forever from returning. In John's vision, a loud voice calls out to the earth and sea, "The devil has come down to you, having great wrath, knowing that he has only a short time" (Revelation

12:12 NASB). What will Satan do since he knows that he has only a brief time left to act? What would you do if you were Satan? He will aggressively pursue the Jewish people, who are fleeing, in an attempt to annihilate every Jew on earth.

"When the dragon realized that he had been thrown down to the earth, he pursued the woman who had given birth to the male child" (12:13). Satan knows that the Jewish people are the key to the second coming of Christ to the earth. Briefly, we will see that if there are no Jewish people on the earth, then the second coming of Christ to earth cannot take place.

Satan desperately pursues Israel beginning at the midpoint of the tribulation. "But she was given two wings like those of a great eagle so she could fly to the place prepared for her in the wilderness. There she would be cared for and protected from the dragon for a time, times, and half a time" (Revelation 12:14).

The "two wings like those of a great eagle" is a symbol of a successful escape through God's help when outnumbered by a powerful enemy. A similar phrase was used for how the Lord miraculously rescued Israel from the Egyptians in the exodus (Exodus 19:4; Deuteronomy 32:11). God will protect and supply the needs of this remnant of Jewish people for a "time, times, and half a time"—the three and a half years of the great tribulation. A place will be prepared in the wilderness ahead of time for the remnant. This place will be discussed in chapter 9.

One might have thought that the Holocaust of World War II would put an end to anti-Semitism. Islamic peoples' hatred for the Jews in modern times should tell us that anti-Semitism will continue to rise. The Bible predicts that during the tribulation there will be another holocaust. Prophecy seems to indicate that in the tribulation as many as two-thirds of all Jewish people in the land of Israel will be killed.

> "Strike down the shepherd, and the sheep will be scattered, and I will turn against the lambs. Two-thirds of the people in the land will be cut off and die," says the LORD. "But one-third will be left

in the land. I will bring that group through the fire and make them pure. I will refine them like silver and purify them like gold. They will call on my name, and I will answer them. I will say, 'These are my people,' and they will say, 'The LORD is our God.'"

Zechariah 13:7–9

The Turning in Israel. The principle of telescoping (a gap of time) separates the first sentence from the second. "Strike down the shepherd" refers to the crucifixion of Jesus, the Good Shepherd (cf. John 10). Jesus was the shepherd of the Jewish people who are now scattered. Sometime after the Jewish people are scattered during the tribulation, "Two-thirds of the people in the land will be cut off and die." But God will preserve one-third, whom he will refine. They will come to faith in Jesus. This will be Israel's turning to the Lord Jesus at the climax of the Seventieth Week of Daniel. Finally they will call on the name of the Lord. The role of the Jewish people calling on the name of the Lord at the second coming to earth will be discussed more fully at the end of this chapter.

The Testimony from Israel. While there will be a great revival among the Jewish people at the very end of the tribulation, many other Jews will come to faith early in the tribulation. For one thing, there will be the 144,000 Jewish evangelists who come to faith very early in the tribulation and begin to give testimony to their faith. Both Revelation 7 and 14 speak of these believers. They are sealed by God on their foreheads (7:3–4) and 12,000 are chosen from each tribe of Israel (7:5–8). Of these 144,000 Jewish believers, Revelation 14:4 states, "They were redeemed from the human race as the firstfruits for God and the Lamb" (HCSB). Another version reads, "They are the first ones to be offered to God and to the Lamb" (TEV).

The firstfruits of a crop in the Jewish culture is a choice sample of the very first yield and was offered back to God in sacrifice. The firstfruits of the harvest gave promise of an even greater harvest to come. The 144,000 give promise that from them will come an even greater harvest of people who will have faith in Jesus. These 144,000 are called God's servants and are sealed for both protection and

99

service. Before John described this vision of the 144,000, he wrote, "Then I saw four angels standing at the four corners of the earth" (Revelation 7:1). The "four corners of the earth" present a worldwide viewpoint (like the four directions on a map). The 144,000 will be Jewish people all over the world, not just Jews living in Israel.

Following the vision of the 144,000, John saw "a vast crowd, too great to count, from every nation and tribe and people and language, standing in front of the throne and before the Lamb" (7:9). In the vision, this crowd was in heaven, not on earth as the 144,000 were. While 144,000 was a precise number, this new group was innumerable. Since they were from "every nation and tribe and people and language," they are primarily Gentiles. Finally, this scene follows the scene of the 144,000 servants of God. The relationship seems to be that the 144,000 have brought this great multitude to faith in Jesus, resulting in eternal life for each one (they are seen in heaven).

John is told the identity of this enormous crowd. "These are the ones who died in the great tribulation. They have washed their robes in the blood of the Lamb and made them white" (7:14). The blood of the Lamb implies the death of Christ. This red blood makes the robes of these martyrs white, symbolic of their spiritual purity before God.

Jesus predicted this worldwide evangelistic movement in his Olivet Discourse. He prophesied, "And the Good News about the Kingdom will be preached throughout the whole world, so that all nations will hear it; and then the end will come" (Matthew 24:14). The "Good News about the Kingdom" includes the message of eternal life by faith in Jesus. It will also include the good news that Jesus is soon to return to earth and set up his rule or kingdom over the world. That's what will take place when he comes to earth again.

The Two Witnesses of Revelation 11

The testimony of Israel also includes the two witnesses described in Revelation 11. God had said to Moses, "The facts of the case must be established by the testimony of two or three witnesses" (Deuteronomy 19:15). Jesus repeated this principle: "It is written that the testimony of two people is true" (John 8:17 ESV). God will supply two witnesses who are mighty prophets to speak to Israel and to the world during the tribulation.

> And I will give power to my two witnesses, and they . . . will prophesy during those 1,260 days. . . . If anyone tries to harm them, fire flashes from their mouths and consumes their enemies. This is how anyone who tries to harm them must die. They have power to shut the sky so that no rain will fall for as long as they prophesy. And they have the power to turn the rivers and oceans into blood, and to strike the earth with every kind of plague as often as they wish.
>
> Revelation 11:3–6

These two Jewish prophets will have the remarkable powers of Moses and Elijah. Moses, of course, was the great leader of Israel who sent plagues from God against the Egyptians, including the turning of the Nile into blood (e.g., Exodus 7:17). Moses fits the description that the two witnesses "turn the rivers and oceans into blood" and "strike the earth with every kind of plague."

Elijah was one of the greatest prophets of the Old Testament. He confronted 950 false prophets of Baal and challenged them to a contest: Whose God could bring down fire from heaven to consume a sacrifice? Elijah prayed, and the God of Israel brought fire down from heaven to consume his sacrifice. The pagan gods failed to do the same, and the prophets of Baal lost their lives (1 Kings 18:19–40). On another occasion, the evil king Ahaziah sent two different detachments of fifty men each to kill Elijah. But the prophet called down fire from heaven each time to destroy the detachments (2 Kings 1:10–12).

Elijah also predicted a drought that would come as a judgment on Israel (1 Kings 18:1). The drought lasted exactly three and a half years (Luke 4:25; James 5:17). Interestingly, the ministry of the two witnesses also takes place for three and a half years, or 1,260 days. At the end of Elijah's ministry, he was taken up mysteriously to heaven without having died (2 Kings 2:11–12). Moses, too, had an unusual death (cf. Jude 9). Both Elijah and Moses appeared to Peter, James, and John when Jesus took them up on the Mount of Transfiguration (Matthew 17:4). They could not have appeared in resurrected bodies. We know this because 1 Corinthians 15:23 says, "But there is an order to this resurrection: Christ was raised as the first of the harvest." No one who died before Christ could have received a resurrected body before Christ was raised from the dead. He was the first to receive a resurrected body.

Many Bible teachers believe that Moses and Elijah will personally return to earth as these two witnesses. God will give them physical bodies again, similar to how Jesus raised Lazarus from the dead (John 11). It may also be because of their testimony that the 144,000 Jewish evangelists come to faith. Whoever these two witnesses are, they will minister in Jerusalem for the first three and a half years of the tribulation. But then the Bible says,

> When they complete their testimony, the beast that comes up out of the bottomless pit will . . . kill them. And their bodies will lie in the main street of Jerusalem . . . the city where their Lord was crucified. And for three and a half days, all peoples, tribes, languages, and nations will stare at their bodies. No one will be allowed to bury them. All the people who belong to this world will gloat over them and give presents to each other to celebrate the death of the two prophets who had tormented them.
>
> Revelation 11:7–10

No one can harm the two witnesses until their testimony is complete. It is the Beast, the Antichrist, who is finally able to kill the two witnesses. This displays the supernatural powers of the Antichrist. He kills the witnesses at the midpoint of the tribulation. The bodies of the two witnesses won't be buried, but somehow, the whole world will be able to stare at their bodies. Today, we realize just how simple that might be with television newscasts. The world of unbelievers ("all the people who belong to this world") will celebrate in a satanic Christmas, giving gifts to each other. They will joyously party because the two witnesses no longer call down plagues on the world's sinful lifestyles.

That's not the end of the story of the two witnesses (or two prophets). God will have the ultimate victory, and so will the two witnesses. "But after three and a half days, God breathed life into them, and they stood up! Terror struck all who were staring at them. Then a loud voice from heaven called to the two prophets, 'Come up here!' And they rose to heaven in a cloud as their enemies watched" (Revelation 11:11–12). The fact that the bodies of the two witnesses lie in Jerusalem for three and a half days subtly prefigures the remaining death-dealing three and a half years of the tribulation.

A Rebuilt Temple in Jerusalem

A Temple for Israel. Although Israel became a nation once again in 1948, it was not until the Six-Day War in 1967 that Israel regained control of the Temple Mount in Jerusalem. The Temple Mount is the large foundation rock on which the first Jewish temple, Solomon's temple, was built. The Babylonians destroyed this temple in their conquest of Israel in 586 BC. A second temple was built by Zerubbabel (515 BC) that remained until the time of Christ. This temple was beautifully adorned at great expense by Herod the Great (d. 4 BC). Ancient historians record how beautiful Herod's temple was. Herod began to elaborately remodel the temple in 20 BC. The beautification of the temple continued until completion in AD 64, just six years before the Romans destroyed the temple. Daniel had predicted this destruction of the temple (9:26). So did Jesus (Mark 13:2).

Only days after the Six-Day War, the actual administration of the Temple Mount in Jerusalem was handed over to the Supreme Muslim Council (the Jerusalem Islamic Waqf), even though the Temple Mount remains to this day within the State of Israel. Israel's concession was made in hopes of keeping peace in Jerusalem. Ongoing conflict results from the fact that the Mosque of Omar (built AD 692), the third most holy Islamic site, sits on what is the thought to be the foundation of the Jewish temple destroyed in AD 70. In Islam, the Mosque of Omar, also called the Dome of the Rock, is considered to house the rock from which Mohammed ascended into heaven.

For several years, Jewish organizations have begun preparations to rebuild the temple so that when the time is right, a third Jewish temple will be erected quickly. High priests have been chosen, their garments have been prepared, and the temple articles of worship have been constructed. No wonder some consider the Temple Mount to be the most volatile thirty-five acres in the world.

Prophecy indicates that a Jewish temple in Jerusalem will exist in the future seven-year tribulation period (Daniel 9:27; Matthew 24:15; 2 Thessalonians 2:4). Since the temple in Jerusalem was destroyed in AD 70, it must be concluded that the Jewish temple in Jerusalem will somehow be rebuilt. Will it be rebuilt before or after the tribulation begins? No prophecy predicts exactly when the temple will be rebuilt. Bible prophecy just describes it as being "there" in the tribulation, but it could be rebuilt many years before the rapture.

Daniel 9:27 tells us that the Antichrist "will put an end to the sacrifices and offerings" in the temple at the middle of the tribulation. The phrase "sacrifices and offerings" is a phrase used in the Old Testament for a fully functioning temple worship. By the midpoint of the tribulation, the temple has been rebuilt for some time. Jesus confirmed this by explaining that "the day is coming when you will see what Daniel the prophet spoke about—the sacrilegious object that causes desecration standing in the Holy Place" (Matthew 24:15). The "Holy Place" refers to the Jerusalem temple.

We also saw previously how the Antichrist, also called the man of lawlessness, asserts his power. "He will exalt himself and defy everything that people call god and every object of worship. He will even sit in the temple of God, claiming that he himself is God" (2 Thessalonians 2:4). This was written by the apostle Paul in the New Testament. Nevertheless, the temple of God must be holy and approved by God. Otherwise, it would not be called the temple of

God. Logically, we must conclude that the two Jewish witnesses in Jerusalem lead the worship in this temple, along with many other Jewish people who have come to faith in Jesus.

Israel at the Second Coming

God told Abraham, "I will make you into a great nation [Israel]. . . . I will bless those who bless you and curse those who treat you with contempt. All the families on earth will be blessed through you" (Genesis 12:2–3). God has never rescinded this promise. Virtually all spiritual blessings have come through the Jewish people. The Bible, including the New Testament, came through the Jews. All the authors of the New Testament, with the exception of Luke, were Jews. The first coming of Christ was through Israel and a Jewish couple, Mary and Joseph. Jesus himself, the Savior of the world, was a Jew. So it should not be surprising that the second coming of Christ to the earth will be the result of the Jewish people as well.

After rebuking the nation for rejecting him as the Messiah, Jesus prophesied the destruction of the Jerusalem temple in AD 70. He announced, "And now, look, your house is abandoned and desolate. For I tell you this, you will never see me again until you say, 'Blessings on the one who comes in the name of the LORD!'" (Matthew 23:38–39). These verses in Matthew 23 are immediately followed by the Olivet Discourse in which Jesus spoke about his return.

The Matthew 23 pronouncement sets up the final condition for the second coming of Christ to the earth. For Jesus to return to earth, the Jewish people as a group must acknowledge Jesus as their Messiah. They will call out to him to come and rescue them from their enemies who are about to destroy them. Then Jesus can return to earth. He will save them from near extermination and destroy all their foes.

Several Bible passages speak of the repentance of Israel and their faith in Jesus as their Messiah at the end times. I mentioned in an earlier chapter that the prophet Zechariah spoke of this Jewish revival. "Then I [the LORD] will pour out a spirit of grace and prayer on the family of David and on the people of Jerusalem. They will look on me whom they have pierced and mourn for him as for an only son. . . . All Israel will mourn" (Zechariah 12:10, 12). In the Hebrew language, the word for "look on" in this passage is a word that indicates faith in Yahweh, the one true God. In the next chapter, Zechariah announced,

> On that day a fountain will be opened for the dynasty of David and for the people of Jerusalem, a fountain to cleanse them from all their sins and impurity. . . . I will refine them like silver and purify them like gold. They will call on my name, and I will answer them. I will say, "These are my people," and they will say, "The LORD is our God."
>
> 13:1, 9

The tribulation will refine the Jewish people, preparing them to *call on the name of the Lord.* This phrase means to call out to the Lord for help in the time of need. The need of the Jewish people at the very end of the tribulation will be to be rescued from the Antichrist and his armies as they attack Jerusalem.

> And I will cause wonders in the heavens and on the earth—blood and fire and columns of smoke. The sun will become dark, and the moon will turn blood red before that great and terrible day of the LORD arrives. But everyone who calls on the name of the LORD will be saved, for some on Mount Zion in Jerusalem will escape, just as the LORD has said. These will be among the survivors whom the LORD has called.
>
> Joel 2:30–32

God will rescue those who call on his name. This is exactly what the Jews will do at the very end of the tribulation. This is also what Paul meant in Romans 11:26, when he said, "All Israel will be saved." Not only will most of the Jewish people come to faith right before Christ's return, they will be delivered or "saved" from their enemies.

8

What Nations Will Be in Power in the End Times?

Many people are curious as to what the Bible says about the United States in the end times. The fact is the Bible says nothing about the United States in the end times. This silence may tell us a few things about the role of the United States in prophecy. While the American culture is rapidly becoming more antagonistic to the Christian faith and the Bible, there are still many Christians throughout the fifty states. Many of these truly believe in Christ as their personal Savior. They are convinced that he is their only hope for heaven. Some of these Christians have significant roles in local or national government, military, industry, technology, medicine, and multiple other roles that directly affect the everyday functioning of the nation. If millions of Christians leave this earth in the rapture, the United States will become an insignificant nation overnight.

It is also possible that America's progressive moral decline and rejection of God will bring his judgment. As a result, the United States might become a weak and irrelevant nation even before the rapture of all true believers takes place. Alternatively, a serious financial crisis or a collapse of the economy due to the nation's debt might cause the downfall of the country. We also know how dependent the United States is on foreign oil. Could an oil crisis be the downfall of America? Some Americans can remember the gasoline crisis in 1970s and the increased gas prices in 2000–2001. America is dependent on the oil reserves of Saudi Arabia. No wonder America

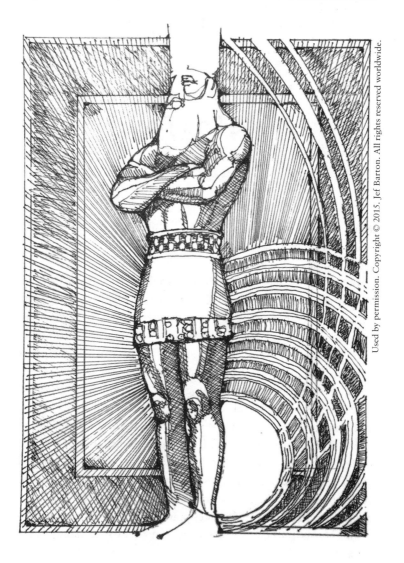

wants to be friends with this nation. Even the military weaponry of the United States is dependent on oil. These factors may explain why the United States is not clearly mentioned in prophecy.

A Powerful Kingdom to Come

Daniel was one of the captives taken to Babylon after King Nebuchadnezzar sieged Israel in 605 BC. In Daniel 2 and 7, five Gentile nations that would control Israel were revealed to Daniel. In chapter 2, these nations were symbolized by a huge humanlike statue in a dream the king had. In chapter 7, the nations were symbolized as strange animals in a dream Daniel had. The two dreams have many parallels. In Nebuchadnezzar's dream, the statue was constructed of various metals. The head of the statue was gold, which represented both King Nebuchadnezzar and his kingdom of Babylon. We learned this principle earlier: The king and the kingdom are often pictured jointly. In a similar way, in Revelation, the beast represents the Antichrist's kingdom, and at other times the Beast represents the Antichrist himself, the individual who rules that kingdom.

In Daniel 2, the statue's chest of silver, waist of bronze, and legs of iron represented the Medo-Persian, Greek, and Roman Empires that would all rule Israel. The iron legs represented the powerful Roman Empire. The Roman Empire was in power during the first coming of Christ. But in the dream revealed to Daniel, there was a second stage of the Roman Empire pictured as the feet with ten toes. The feet with ten toes were a mixture of iron and clay, not just iron. This alone suggests a different stage of the Roman Empire. The ten toes represent ten contemporaneous kings. Nothing in the history of the ancient Roman Empire matches the stage where there were ten concurrent kings ruling the Empire.

The stage of the ten toes predicts a Roman Empire II in the end times. Once again, there is a gap of time between the stage of the iron legs (basically, the first coming of Christ), and the stage of the feet with ten toes (the second coming of Christ to earth).

The legs of the statue were iron, but the feet and toes were both iron and clay (v. 42). Daniel was told in the interpretation of the dream that this kingdom will have some strength (iron) and some weakness (clay), and that "the people will be a mixture and will not remain united" (Daniel 2:43 NIV).

Many Bible interpreters understand verse 43 to mean that the future revived Roman Empire will include a mixture of people with different languages and cultures. These languages and cultures will make it difficult for the empire to be unified. Europe is certainly a mixture of languages and cultures. If the ancient Roman Empire were to be renewed, it could also include all or parts of Turkey, Syria, Lebanon, Iraq, and North Africa.

After Daniel saw the feet and toes in the vision, he saw a rock cut out of a mountain, but not by human hands. This rock crushed the entire statue (not just the feet), symbolizing the complete destruction of all earthly kingdoms. The rock represents the Lord Jesus. Many Bible passages identify Jesus as the Rock. The book of 1 Peter, quoting from Isaiah, says of Jesus, "He is the stone that makes people stumble, the rock that makes them fall" (2:8). Daniel is told further, "During the reigns of those [ten] kings, the God of heaven will set up a kingdom that will never be destroyed or conquered. It will crush all these kingdoms into nothingness, and it will stand forever" (Daniel 2:44). The kingdom of God will be set up at the coming of Jesus to the earth. The kingdom he brings "will crush all these [other] kingdoms into nothingness."

There is a spiritual, invisible kingdom that coexists beside earthly kingdoms today. Churches often talk about this spiritual kingdom. The kingdom of God in Daniel 2 is a future, earthly kingdom that will replace all other earthly kingdoms. This messianic kingdom is revealed further in Revelation 20 (see chapter 11, "What Is the Millennium?"). Daniel 2 implies that the destruction of all these earthly kingdoms will be sudden, violent, immediate, thorough, and political.

By political, I mean that Jesus will rule as king over the earth much like earthly kings rule, only with justice and righteousness.

His form of government will not be a democracy, i.e., a rule by the people. It will be a dictatorship—but with a dictator who is all-knowing, all-loving, all-just, and all-righteous. Daniel 2:35 depicts Jesus taking over the world governments: "The whole statue was crushed into small pieces of iron, clay, bronze, silver, and gold. Then the wind blew them away without a trace, like chaff on a threshing floor. But the rock that knocked the statue down became a great mountain that covered the whole earth."

In the Bible, a mountain is sometimes an image for a kingdom, as it is in Daniel 2. This will help later in interpreting a key passage in Revelation. In Daniel 2, the "great mountain" is the kingdom Jesus will set up. The destruction of the statue represents the powerful appearance of Jesus at his second coming to earth. It is then he will overcome the worldwide kingdom of the evil dictator, the Antichrist, and replace it with his righteous rule over the earth.

Roman Empire II and Its Ten Kings

The Antichrist's kingdom will be composed of ten kings and their nations, pictured as the ten toes of the statue. The toes are kings and their kingdoms. In the interpretation of the statue, Daniel was told, "This mixture of iron and clay [in the feet and toes] also shows that *these kingdoms* will try to strengthen themselves. . . . During *the reigns of those kings*, the God of heaven will set up a kingdom. . . . It will crush all *these kingdoms* into nothingness" (Daniel 2:43–44, italics added). These ten kings will rule at the same time under the Antichrist right before Jesus returns to earth and takes over the government(s) of the world.

This interpretation of Daniel 2 is confirmed by similar prophecies in Daniel 7. The prophecies of the two dreams in these two chapters can help interpret each other. Most of the Old Testament was written in the Hebrew language. Only small portions were written in Aramaic. Aramaic was the primary language of the

Babylonians, who were Gentiles. In the original manuscripts of Daniel, Daniel 2:4 switches from Hebrew to Aramaic. These manuscripts conclude the Aramaic section at the last verse in chapter 7. All other sections of Daniel are in Hebrew.

Daniel 2 and 7 begin and end the section in Aramaic. Why this change of languages? A reasonable suggestion is that Daniel 2–7 focuses on Gentile nations that rule over Israel—in the past and in the future. Hebrew is the language of the Jews. The sections of Daniel in Hebrew focus on the Jewish people and their final deliverance at Jesus' return to earth. All of this helps us understand that chapters 2 and 7 may be designed to correspond to each other. The whole section of Daniel 2–7 has parallels. Chapters 2 and 7 contain two dreams. Chapters 3 and 6 are rescue stories (the fiery furnace and the lions' den). Chapters 4 and 5 are stories about God's judgment on pride (Nebuchadnezzar and Belshazzar).

Daniel 2 and 7 Parallels

World Empire	Daniel 2	Daniel 7
Babylon	Head of Gold	Lion with Eagles Wings
Medo-Persia	Chest and Arms of Silver	Bear Raised Up on One Side
Greece	Belly and Thighs of Bronze	Leopard with Four Wings and Four Heads
Rome	Legs of Iron	Terrifying Beast with Iron Teeth
Rome II	Ten Toes	Ten Horns, Little Horn

Like Daniel 2, Daniel 7 also depicts a future Roman Empire with ten kings who rule at the same time. The four beasts that Daniel saw in his dream in Daniel 7 describe the same nations as revealed in Daniel 2. Just as the fourth metal (iron) in the statue of Daniel 2 was Rome, so the fourth beast of Daniel 7 is Rome. "Then in my vision that night, I saw a fourth beast—terrifying, dreadful, and very strong. It devoured and crushed its victims with huge iron teeth and trampled their remains beneath its feet. It was different from any of the other beasts, and it had ten horns" (Daniel 7:7). The fourth beast's iron teeth remind us of the iron legs of the statue in Daniel 2. The fourth beast's crushing feet remind us of the feet and toes of the statue. Finally, the ten horns in Daniel 7 remind us of the ten toes in Daniel 2.

Daniel saw a "little horn" rise up among the ten horns of the fourth beast. The little horn became prominent and began boasting arrogantly. He "came up afterward and destroyed three of the other horns. This horn had seemed greater than the others" (Daniel 7:20). As the dream is interpreted for Daniel, it becomes evident that the Little Horn of Daniel 7 is the Antichrist. But before the future Antichrist rises to power, a revived Roman Empire of ten unified nations will be in existence.

In Daniel's dream, he watched as the Ancient One (God) in heaven, attended by millions of angels, judged the Little Horn and destroyed his kingdom. Then Daniel saw "someone like a son of man coming with the clouds of heaven" (7:13). This "son of man" was given authority to rule forever over all the nations of the world. The *Son of Man* is a title for the Messiah.

Every Bible interpreter, from the most skeptical to the most conservative, agrees that Daniel 7:13 is the source of Jesus' use of the title *Son of Man* for himself. In the New Testament, the Son of Man is not used primarily to describe Jesus' humanity. It is used of his right to return to earth, to judge the world, and set up his kingdom in the end times, just like Daniel 7 describes. Jesus used the title *Son of Man* in the prophecies of the Olivet Discourse more than in any other section of the four gospels. For example, in Matthew 24:30, he said, "And they will see the Son of Man coming on the clouds of heaven with power and great glory."

Earlier I suggested that *horns* in Scripture were symbols of strength and power, such as the power of a great ruler. In some contexts, such as Daniel 7, *horns* may suggest military strength. The ten horns in Daniel 7 represent ten powerful kings/kingdoms. Daniel was told,

> This fourth beast is the fourth world power that will rule the earth. . . .
> Its ten horns are ten kings who will rule that empire. Then another

> king will arise, different from the other ten, who will subdue three of
> them. He will defy the Most High and oppress the holy people of the
> Most High. He will try to change their sacred festivals and laws, and
> they will be placed under his control for a time, times, and half a time.
>
> 7:23–25

The phrase "a time, times, and half a time" points to three and a half years of the seven-year tribulation. Is this the first or the second three and a half years of the tribulation?

Since the Little Horn will "oppress the holy people of the Most High," this is the great tribulation, or the second three and a half years. It is during the second half of Daniel's Seventieth Week that the Little Horn will persecute the Jews. The actual ten kings and the Antichrist will arise early in the tribulation. Daniel tells us that as the Antichrist rises to power, not all of the nations in Roman Empire II will quickly submit to his leadership. He will need to "subdue three of them." Perhaps these kings will be killed and replaced by other kings. Then the ten kings/kingdoms will rule under the Antichrist.

Since the Little Horn will attempt to change the "sacred festivals and laws" of the people of God, it seems likely he will do away with our calendar system of BC (before Christ) and AD (*Anno Domini*, in the year of our Lord). Undoubtedly, he will outlaw the celebrations of Christmas and Easter as well. Worst of all, "He will defy the Most High" (i.e., the God of the Bible).

Just as in Daniel 2 and 7, Revelation also pictures the ten kings as ruling with the Antichrist in the tribulation. "The ten horns of the beast [Roman Empire II] are ten kings who have not yet risen to power. They will be appointed to their kingdoms for one brief moment to reign with the beast [the Antichrist]" (Revelation 17:12). In this verse, the first use of the word *beast* refers to the final kingdom of the world; the second use refers to the final king of the world (apart from Christ).

Finally, in the interpretation of Daniel's dream, the "holy people" were also given authority to co-rule with the Son of

Man, and God's eternal kingdom was set up in its first stage: a kingdom over this earth as we now know it. "But then the court will pass judgment, and all his [i.e., the Little Horn's] power will be taken away and completely destroyed. Then the sovereignty, power, and greatness of all the kingdoms under heaven will be given to the holy people of the Most High. His kingdom will last forever, and all rulers will serve and obey him" (Daniel 7:26–27).

Implications of the Roman Empire II

Numerous European leaders in past history have visualized a revived Roman Empire. The pope crowned Charlemagne, King of the Franks, as "Emperor of the Romans" on Christmas Day, AD 800. Napoleon longed to form a united federation of Europe, claiming, "I am a Roman emperor in the best line of the Caesars." Wilhelm I, first German emperor (1871–1888), was given the title *Kaiser*, German for Caesar. Hitler declared that the Roman Empire had been revived through Mussolini (1883–1945).

In 1957, the European Economic Community was formed at an assembly in Rome. In 1993, the European Union was formed, and by 2009, the European Union incorporated the EEC's agenda under its wider purposes. The EU is a political and economic coalition of nations. Many Christians have been watching the EU closely. Could the European Union be the fulfillment of the prophesied ten nations of the revived Roman Empire? At one time, there were only ten nations in the EU (1981–1985). This aroused the speculations that the EU would be the fulfillment of Daniel's prophecy. Then the number of nations joining the EU continued to grow. In 2015, the EU reached twenty-eight nations. This demonstrates the need to be cautious about interpreting current events as if they were the fulfillment of Bible prophecy.

On the other hand, it is still possible that the EU is the beginning stage of the prophecies of Daniel and Revelation regarding the future Roman Empire. As of 2014, the EU generated a gross domestic product bigger than any other country. The euro has taken hold as the EU's legal tender for many of the nations in the EU. The most we can say is that the EU is very interesting in light of Bible prophecy.

Years ago, I remember reading the printed lectures of several speakers at Bible prophecy conferences in America in the early 1900s. They referred to the prophecies in the Bible that the Jews would one day be in their own land in preparation for the second coming of Christ. I can imagine that many people at the time who didn't believe the Bible would have ridiculed how these Christians interpreted Bible prophecy. Israel miraculously became a nation again in 1948 in fulfillment of prophecy. Some may scoff at the thought of a Roman Empire II. Like the now-fulfilled prophecy of the return of the nation of Israel to its land in 1948, one day there will be a revived confederacy of the Roman Empire led by the Antichrist. The ancient Roman Empire will rise again.

When the wicked character of Adolph Hitler became clear to the world, many Christians viewed him as the Antichrist. They were wrong, of course. However, Satan *may* have been fully intending to use Hitler as the Antichrist. I'm sure that Satan has attempted to use others in past history as his dictator or king over the whole earth. The devil longs to prove God's Scriptures in error, including when and how the Antichrist appears and rises to power. But God is in full control of world events. He will not allow the demonic forces to bring the Antichrist on the scene before his prophesied time.

In the same way, Satan may be working hard to bring about the world powers that will support the Antichrist. If it is not God's time for them, those powers may look like the fulfillment of prophecy at first, but then collapse and show us that the fulfillment is yet to come. Maybe, but only maybe, the EU will become the Roman Empire II.

Prophecies About Islamic Nations

Some of the most difficult prophecies to interpret are the prophecies of Ezekiel 38–39. Yet the chapters are clear enough in their message to determine that nothing in past history has come close to fulfilling the predictions here. Both chapters describe a sudden attack against Israel from various surrounding nations. Many Bible interpreters understand the two chapters to be a repetition of the same prophecy, not two different events. Chapter 39 repeats, overlaps, or gives a flashback in order to add details to chapter 38. As mentioned earlier, this is a valid principle in Scripture that explains how some prophecies are arranged. I am not confident that these two chapters use this principle. Since this is one of the most well-accepted views among Bible prophecy experts, I will explain these chapters from this viewpoint.

Ezekiel was a young priest who was exiled to Babylon in the second deportation of King Nebuchadnezzar (597 BC), when the Babylonians conquered Israel. Daniel was taken captive from Jerusalem to Babylon in the first deportation (586 BC). There is no clear evidence that Daniel and Ezekiel ever met. They lived in different communities. But Ezekiel was well aware of Daniel's life and character in Babylon and mentioned his righteousness along with that of Noah and Job (Ezekiel 14:14, 20; 28:3). Ezekiel's original listeners and readers would have been the Jewish people in the Babylonian captivity.

Ezekiel 38 and 39 describe a violent attack against Israel while the Jews are living securely in their own land. God prophesies to the invaders, "In the distant future you will swoop down on the land of Israel, which will be enjoying peace after recovering from war and after its people have returned from many lands to the mountains of Israel" (38:8). This description of Israel appears to be possible only after the reestablishment of the nation in 1948. That's the clear impression we get from "after its people have returned from many lands to the mountains of Israel."

117

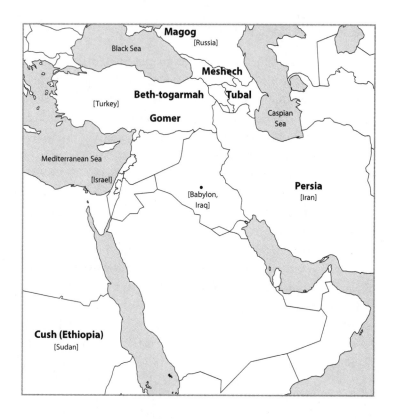

Both chapters begin by addressing "Gog, of the land of Magog, the chief prince of Meshech and Tubal" (Ezekiel 38:2 HCSB). God warns Gog, "I am your enemy!" (v. 3). Gog is the ruler of the ancient people groups of Magog, Meshech, and Tubal. The title *Gog* is a title like caesar, president, or prime minister rather than a personal name. These people groups described as Magog, Meshech, and Tubal lived in what is today the very southern portion of Russia between the Caspian and Black Seas, and perhaps in what is now the northeastern corner of Turkey as well.

The Hebrew word for "chief" could be a proper name, *Rosh*, adding another country to the list. The Ezekiel 38 reference in the NASB reads, "the prince of *Rosh*" instead of "the *chief* prince." Interpreting Rosh as either an adjective (*chief*) or as a proper name

(*Rosh*) is something like the use of our word *joy*. It could describe an emotion or it could be a person's name.

Many interpreters trace the proper name *Rosh* to people groups in portions of southern Russia. Although the name sounds similar to the word *Russia*, identifying Rosh is based on the studies of ancient peoples, not phonetic similarity. There is another clue to the fact that many of these countries come from geographical territories governed today by Russia. Three times Ezekiel describes these nations as coming from "the distant north" (38:6, 15; 39:2). It is easy to see on a map that Russia is located directly to the distant north of Israel and Jerusalem.

Even more nations or territories (38:5–6) are added to the list of those who will attack Israel. Ezekiel adds that "many others" are with Gog. Some names of the nations depend on the Bible translation used. In the battle against Israel, Ezekiel also includes armies from Persia (modern Iran), Ethiopia or Cush (modern Sudan), Libya or Put (modern Libya), Gomer (central Turkey), and Beth-togarmah or "house of Togarmah" (northeastern Turkey). Altogether, many or most of the territories described in this prophecy are Islamic by religion today. Again, in light of the ongoing conflict between Israel and Islamic nations today, it is intriguing to see a prophetic passage that seems to suggest warfare between these two religious groups.

These hostile nations will attack Israel with "horses and charioteers in full armor and a great horde armed with shields and swords" (Ezekiel 38:4). This weaponry presents a challenge to the interpretation of prophecy. Are we to understand that these armies will attack Israel with ancient weapons, not modern weapons? There are two possible solutions. First, perhaps at this time in the future, there will be such a radical disarmament that the only military weapons available will be ancient weaponry, stockpiled in secrecy. Second, it could be that Ezekiel and other prophecies use language appropriate for their cultures rather than describing tanks and machine guns that would be totally meaningless to their original listeners and readers.

One of the reasons for this invasion will certainly be the hatred of the Jews by the invaders. Many Islamic fundamentalists maintain the ideology that the Jewish people are infidels who must be killed and their nation not allowed to exist. Anti-Semitism has existed ever since the Jewish people became a nation, long before Islam's beginnings in the seventh century AD. The Lord, through Ezekiel, gives another motivation for this invasion: greed and materialism. These invading warriors say, "I will capture vast amounts of plunder, for the people are rich with livestock and other possessions now" (Ezekiel 38:12).

When Will This Islamic Invasion Occur?

This is the most debated question. The battle has been placed at almost every point in the prophetic future: (1) before the tribulation; (2) between the rapture and the tribulation (some interpreters see a time gap between these two events); (3) at the midpoint of the tribulation; (4) at the end of the tribulation; (5) at the beginning of the one-thousand-year kingdom of Christ on earth; and (6) at the end of that one-thousand-year kingdom. I will explain the midtribulation perspective.

This position maintains that the key to when this invasion takes place is the reference to Israel living securely in its own land. The invaders from the north will say, "Israel is an unprotected land filled with unwalled villages! I will march against her and destroy these people who live in such confidence!" (Ezekiel 38:11). The primary time this false security will take place is during the first half of the tribulation. It is at this time that the Antichrist will make a treaty with Israel to protect it from invasion. He will assure the Jewish people that he himself and his new Roman Empire II will defend them against any aggressors.

This is also a time when Israel as a whole nation has not yet turned to the Messiah in faith. After God supernaturally destroys these enemies, many Jewish people will come to faith in Jesus.

God promises that "from that time on the people of Israel will know that I am the LORD their God" (Ezekiel 39:22). Some of the Jewish people will begin to respond with faith in Jesus as their Messiah in the first half of the tribulation under the ministry of the two witnesses in Jerusalem. At the midpoint of the tribulation, many more will come to faith and flee Jerusalem when they see the abomination that causes desolation. The greatest response among the Jewish people will come at the end of the tribulation. That will totally fulfill Ezekiel 39:22. This invasion must take place sometime before the climax of the tribulation.

What destruction will this Islamic assault inflict on Israel? Absolutely none! God declares that he will intervene for his people and defeat their adversaries. First, God says, "I swear in My zeal and fiery rage: On that day there will be a great earthquake in the land of Israel" (Ezekiel 38:19 HCSB). Second, this earthquake apparently leads to pandemonium among the troops so that they turn on each other. The different raiding nations, which will have different languages, will begin fighting against each other (v. 21). Today, the languages of these countries include at least Russian, Farsi, Arabic, and Turkish. In God's sovereign design, the infighting will be radically self-defeating. Third, God will send more devastating disasters such as "disease and bloodshed . . . torrential rain, hailstones, fire, and burning sulfur!" (v. 22).

If an Islamic invasion takes place just before the midpoint of the tribulation, the Antichrist may use the opportunity to break his covenant with Israel. Since many of the rival powers to his revived Roman Empire (e.g., Russia) will be supernaturally eliminated in this warfare, he may take full credit for the defeat of his enemies and begin his claim to deity.

Another group of nations, and a significant leading city, will also be instrumental in the end-times warfare in Israel. These prophecies will be discussed in the next chapter.

121

9

What Is Armageddon?

When most people hear the word *Armageddon,* they usually think of a global war that brings an end to human life and civilization. The Armageddon in the Bible takes place at the very end of the tribulation period, just as Jesus returns to earth, and it doesn't end civilization or life on the earth.

Actually, the Bible uses the word *Armageddon* only once—in Revelation 16:16. There it is not used as a title of the final war on earth but as a description of the *place* where the armies of the final war gather. It states, "And the demonic spirits gathered all the rulers and their armies to a place with the Hebrew name *Armageddon.*"

The actual final world war is not given a precise name. Nor does its description emphasize only an international conflict. What is emphasized is that the battle will be a warfare led by the rulers or kings of the earth, deceived by the Antichrist. They will move toward Jerusalem to fight against Jesus, the Lord of heaven and earth. Revelation states that demonic spirits work miracles and "go out to all the rulers of the world to gather them *for battle against the Lord* on that great judgment day of God the Almighty" (Revelation 16:14). This battle will be a battle fought by the Antichrist's worldwide armies against the Lord Jesus as he comes with his armies from heaven to earth. Other Bible versions call the battle in this verse "the battle of the great day of God, the Almighty."

Where is Armageddon located? The Hebrew word *Armageddon* actually means "mountain (or hill) of Megiddo." Megiddo was an ancient northern city of Israel but is a deserted mound today. The very small "mountain" (or hill) at Megiddo is certainly not big enough for an assembly of armies. The broad plain or widespread valley associated with the hill of Megiddo certainly is. This flat, open valley is located about fifty miles north of Jerusalem (or about twenty miles south-southeast of Haifa). In the Old Testament, Israel fought several battles against their enemies on this plain.

The worldwide armies gather against the Lord Jesus at Armageddon, but they do not fight there. From the plains of Megiddo where they gather, the armies will march against Jerusalem. That's where much of the world's final warfare will take place. The Old Testament prophets Daniel, Joel, and Zechariah all predict that Jerusalem will be the location of the final battle on earth. For example, Zechariah 12:3 quotes the Lord's perspective of this battle: "On that day I will make Jerusalem an immovable rock. All the nations will gather against it to try to move it, but they will only hurt themselves." The phrase *all the nations* implies that this is not a historical (past) attack on Jerusalem but a prophetic (future) one.

Nazi Germany perceived the Jews to be a detriment to the progress of society. In a similar way, the people of the earth in the end times will be deceived into thinking that the Jews are the source of all the world's problems. So the Antichrist, controlled by Satan, will attempt to purge the world of the Jews.

The God of This World

According to the Gospels, after Jesus had fasted for forty days, Satan tempted him three times. The third time, Satan took Jesus up to the peak of a very high mountain and showed him all the kingdoms of the world and all their glory. Satan said to Jesus, "I will give it all to you . . . if you will kneel down and worship me" (Matthew 4:9). But Jesus rejected Satan's offer. Was the devil's offer a sham? How could Satan give "all the kingdoms of the world" to Jesus if these kingdoms were never Satan's to give in the first place? They were Satan's kingdoms to give. The temptation was authentic; the offer was not bogus.

When God created people, he gave to Adam and Eve and their offspring the responsibility to rule over creation. God said to the first couple, "Be fruitful and multiply. Fill the earth and govern it" (Genesis 1:28). That privilege of governing the world was forfeited when Adam and Eve sinned. Satan, who led them into sin, became the ruler of the kingdoms of the earth instead. Both Jesus (John 12:31; 16:11) and Paul (Ephesians 2:2) spoke of Satan as the ruler and god of this world. When Jesus rejected Satan's offer to become the devil's human instrument to rule the earth, Satan began his search for another person to take up his offer. The Antichrist will be that person.

The conflict between good and evil will climax at the "battle of the great day of God, the Almighty" (Revelation 16:14 HCSB). Will the Antichrist and Satan maintain their hold as rulers of this world? Or will Jesus and God the Father take over the earth and its kingdoms? Christians know the answer and they follow the Victor. Satan and the Antichrist will not be the rulers of the world. At Jesus' coming to the earth, he will take over the world as its final ruler forever.

Stage #1: The Gathering of the World's Armies

World War II was made up of various individual conflicts, such as the Battle of the Bulge and the Battle of Normandy (D-Day). Similarly, many Christian teachers call the final war on earth the Campaign of Armageddon, not the "war of Armageddon." This is because the final war on earth describes a series of military operations or conflicts rather than describing a single battle. There are at least eight stages of the Campaign of Armageddon.

For the final, decisive battle in World War II (D-Day, June 6, 1944), the allied troops of the United States, Canada, and England assembled in Great Britain. The battle itself was fought on a fifty-mile stretch of French coastline named Normandy. In a similar manner, the Antichrist will gather his worldwide forces at Armageddon (stage #1). It appears from Scripture that they will march against three locations. They will move against Babylon in the east (stage #2) and Jerusalem in the south (stage #3). The fight at Jerusalem will be in the Valley of Jehoshaphat, also called the Kidron Valley. They will also storm against a remnant of Jews in a city called Bozrah (stage #4).

In the Old Testament, Armageddon, the hill and city of Megiddo that overlooks the large valley next to it, was also called the Valley of Jezreel. This plain is twenty miles long and fourteen miles wide. A great military victory was accomplished in the Jezreel Valley when Gideon defeated the armies of the Midianites with just three hundred men (Judges 7). Perhaps Israel, as led by Gideon, so greatly outnumbered in the battle with their enemies, points in anticipation to the future war against Israel in the end times. Seemingly overpowered and outnumbered, the Jews at the climax of the tribulation will supernaturally win the final victory in the "battle of the great day of God, the Almighty."

The name *Jezreel* means "God sows." After the defeat of Israel's enemies, God will gather his believing Jewish people and will "sow" or plant them in his land once again. In 722 BC, Assyria conquered Israel's northern tribes (the territories called Samaria and Galilee in the New Testament), and separated them from the southern tribes (the territory called Judea). But God promised that the northern and southern tribes would be reunited as a single nation in the last days. "Then the people of Judah and Israel will unite together. They will choose one leader for themselves [the Messiah Jesus], and they will return from exile together. What a day that will be—the day of Jezreel—when God will again plant his people in his land" (Hosea 1:11).

This gathering of a united Jewish people was also mentioned by Jesus in his Olivet Discourse when he spoke of his coming to earth. "And he [the Son of Man] will send out his angels with the mighty blast of a trumpet, and they will gather his [Jewish] chosen ones from all over the world—from the farthest ends of the earth and heaven" (Matthew 24:31). Every Jew who is still living at the coming of Christ to the earth and has come to faith in Jesus will be brought back to the land of Israel to begin rulership with Jesus over the earth for one thousand years.

During stage #1 of the Armageddon campaign, vast armies of the world, led by "all the rulers of the world" (Revelation 16:14), will gather at Armageddon. In the announcement of the sixth bowl judgment of Revelation, the "kings from the east" are singled out. It is also within the description of the sixth bowl judgment that the word *Armageddon* appears. "Then the sixth angel poured out his bowl on the great Euphrates River, and it dried up so that the kings from the east could march their armies toward the west without hindrance. And I saw three evil spirits that looked like frogs leap from the mouths of the dragon, the beast, and the false prophet" (Revelation 16:12–13). These demons go out "from the mouths" of the dragon (Satan), the Beast (the Antichrist), and the False Prophet. Christians sometimes call these three the false trinity because they imitate the authentic Trinity. Along with satanic miracles, exceedingly deceptive words ("from the mouths") will induce the kings of the east to gather at Armageddon for their fight with Jerusalem and with Jesus.

The "kings from the east" are often interpreted to be armies coming from China and other countries of the Far East. China is certainly to the east of Jerusalem and Israel. But "east" in the Bible is primarily Mesopotamia, the territories surrounding the two rivers, the Tigris and the Euphrates. Today, Mesopotamia is mostly eastern Iraq, western Iran, eastern Syria, and southeastern Turkey. It is not impossible in prophecy for the "kings [plural] of the east" to extend much farther, including more distant lands, perhaps even as far as China.

What Does Revelation Mean by "Babylon the Great"?

Before discussing stage #2 of the Armageddon campaign, we need to identify "Babylon the Great" in the book of Revelation. Babylon the Great is the end-time city that will be radically anti-God and anti-Christian. About one out of every ten verses in Revelation concerns the subject of the city of Babylon. Next to Jerusalem, the Bible refers to Babylon more than any other city. Ancient Babylon is located about fifty miles south of modern Baghdad. Most of the ancient city of Babylon is in ruins today. How can the book of Revelation speak about the city of Babylon in the end times?

One view is that Babylon is not to be interpreted as a literal city. Instead, *Babylon* is thought to be a symbol for everything that stands against the true God. Las Vegas, Nevada, is also a symbol of certain earthly values, but Las Vegas is more than a symbolic name; it is a real city as well. The Babylon of Revelation is more than a symbol of anti-God values. It is also an actual city where anti-God values are centered and radically promoted.

Another interpretation of *Babylon* is that it is a code name in Revelation for the first-century city of Rome. Rome, of course, was the powerful pagan capital of the Roman Empire during the time of Jesus and the writing of Revelation. First-century Rome was well-known for its persecution of Christians. It is suggested that if *Babylon* was a code name for Rome, this would protect the writer and any of his readers from charges of treason against the Roman Empire. For if Revelation condemned Rome outright, anyone caught with a copy of the book would certainly be martyred.

The apostle John usually makes it clear when he wants us to understand that a city is symbolic. For example, he writes "Jerusalem, the city that is figuratively called 'Sodom' and 'Egypt,' the city where their Lord was crucified" (Revelation 11:8). Here John's wording makes it clear that *Sodom* and *Egypt* are symbolic names for the city of Jerusalem.

If *Babylon* is a cryptic or mystery name in Revelation for ancient or future Rome, how do we interpret the references in Revelation to the Euphrates River? The Euphrates River is the Mesopotamian river that flowed through Babylon. Revelation 16:12 says, "The sixth angel poured out his bowl on the great Euphrates River, and it dried up so that the kings from the east could march their armies toward the west without hindrance." If *Babylon* is a symbol for Rome, should we interpret the Euphrates River as the Tiber River that flows through Rome? If so, where is the "west" to which the kings of the east are marching? There are only fourteen miles (22.5 km) of land to the west of Rome before one reaches the Mediterranean Sea.

Revelation 17:9 describes Babylon as a harlot who sits on seven hills. "The seven heads are seven hills on which the woman sits" (NIV). Many Bible interpreters understand the "seven hills" in Revelation 17:9 to mean the seven hills of Rome on which the city is situated. The woman "sitting" on the seven hills does not designate the woman's location but her control. In Revelation 17:3, John saw "a woman sitting on a scarlet beast that . . . had seven heads and ten horns." These heads and horns are kingdoms and kings. Again, the woman "sitting" on the Beast portrays the woman's control, not her location. In other words, the city of Babylon controls these kingdoms and kings.

The original Greek word for "hills" in the phrase "seven hills on which the woman sits" (NIV) can also be translated *mountains*. In our discussion of Daniel 2, it was pointed out that a mountain often refers to kings or kingdoms. The rest of Revelation 17:9 (in some versions, v. 10) reads, "They [the hills or mountains] also represent seven kings." The seven mountains on which the woman sits are seven kings/kingdoms that the city of Babylon controls. The seven hills are not the seven hills of the city of Rome.

In Revelation 17:1, one of the seven angels who had the seven bowls instructs John, "Come, I will show you the punishment of the great prostitute, who sits by many waters" (NIV). What does it mean that the prostitute sits by many waters? Is this her location? Not likely. A few verses later we are given the divine interpretation of the prostitute sitting by many waters. "The waters you saw, where the prostitute sits, are peoples, multitudes, nations and languages" (Revelation 17:15 NIV). The prostitute (the city of Babylon) is not located on people. That makes no sense. The act of sitting is described as the control the city (the prostitute) has over the people of the world.

Babylon Means Babylon

The best interpretation of *Babylon* in the book of Revelation is to understand it as the same ancient city that was once an arch-enemy of Israel. While Babylon lies mostly in ruins today, Satan will seek to rebuild this ancient city that once stood as the chief representation of sin and evil in the world.

The garden of Eden, where humanity first began, was located near the Euphrates River. The beginning of humanity was in this central area of the world. Humans were told to spread out from this area in the Middle East (Genesis 1:22, 28; 2:14). People became so sinful and so violent that God judged the world by a flood (Genesis 6:11). Yet in his grace, God protected righteous Noah and his family by means of the ark that Noah built in obedience to God.

About one hundred years after the flood, several descendants of Noah founded a city under the leadership of Nimrod. In Hebrew, *Nimrod* means "We will rebel." While God had commanded people to spread through the earth, Nimrod and other defiant people united together to build a city. This was an expression of their rebellion against God's command to spread through the earth. The city quickly became a center for false worship and idolatry. The inhabitants built a tower in Babylonia (also called the land of Shinar) to reach up to heaven and to God. They wanted to make a name for themselves (Genesis 11:4). The tower was called the Tower of Babel. *Babel* is the origin of the name Babylon.

It's commonly believed that the Tower of Babel was an ancient ziggurat. A ziggurat was a temple-tower built on top of several massive rectangular-shaped platforms, one on top of the other.

At each ascending level, the platforms became smaller, forming a pyramid shape. Stairways allowed for access to the temple at the top. These temple-towers were common in ancient Mesopotamia. A ziggurat dated from 2100 BC is found in the ancient city of Ur on the Euphrates River about one hundred fifty miles (247 km) southeast of Babylon.

In the garden of Eden, Adam and Eve succumbed to the temptation to be like God (Genesis 3:5). The building of the Tower of Babel was also an attempt to become like God. In irony, the Bible tells us that God had to "come down" to see the tower. No human tower—or human religion—could ever reach the true God. After the flood, the people of the earth were all descendants of Noah, so naturally they all spoke the same language. This made it easier for them to come together in rebellion against the true God. God confused the languages people spoke. Since people now spoke many different languages, they were forced to spread out on the earth and were less able to unite in worldwide false worship. Our English word *babel* is based on this biblical event when God confused human languages.

The evil beginning of the city of Babylon also sets its pattern for the end times. As described in Revelation, the Babylon of the end times is also a wicked, anti-God force in the world. Because Babylon's worldliness, sinful pleasures, and moral decadence will allure the people of the world to join in these evil pleasures, Babylon is portrayed as a seductive harlot. The apostle John described Babylon as a prostitute who has given birth to and mothered other prostitutes (i.e., other false religions and anti-God powers in the world). Revelation 17:5 calls her, "Babylon the Great, Mother of All Prostitutes and Obscenities in the World."

Spiritual intimacy must be between each person and the true God of the Bible. Spiritual prostitution describes one who is unfaithful to God by a devotion to self or other gods. These gods may be personal or impersonal. While spiritual prostitution often pictures idolatry in the Old Testament, it also portrays the misuse for one's own personal gain of all that God has created. All earthly pleasures, even good ones, can be prostituted when not used in honor of the one true God of the Bible and Jesus his Son.

Jerusalem is the city of God. Throughout the Bible, it is described as where God has chosen to reside. According to Revelation, in the future, God will build a New Jerusalem for his followers. The New Jerusalem is called a bride. Have you ever seen an ugly bride? Not likely. Every bride makes herself amazingly attractive. In other words, the New Jerusalem will be absolutely beautiful. Satan will attempt to build an imitation of the New Jerusalem— a "New Babylon" for his followers like the Babylon of old. The city of God is Jerusalem. Babylon will be the city of Satan, so this woman (the city of Babylon) is called a prostitute.

Why Will the City of Babylon Be Rebuilt?

Ancient Babylonia and its capital, Babylon, were the evil empire and capital city that in 605 BC conquered Israel and exiled thousands of Jewish people to Babylon. Seventy years later, King Cyrus of the Medo-Persian Empire conquered Babylon almost overnight. At the time, very little of the city was destroyed. In the book of Daniel, we are told that this godly Jew, Daniel, was immediately given a position of leadership in Babylon under the new Persian rule. Life in Babylon proceeded almost as usual (Daniel 5:30–6:2). Babylon was not destroyed suddenly or completely. Its significance merely faded over time.

In 334 BC, at age twenty-two, Alexander the Great conquered Babylon for the Greek Empire and made it one of his capitals. One of the following Greek rulers built a city named Seleucia, fifty-six miles (90 km) north of Babylon, and transferred most of the inhabitants of Babylon to Seleucia. Although the glory of Babylon faded away through the centuries, Babylon continued to exist. In the New Testament, we learn of a large group of Jews that came from Mesopotamia (the area of Babylon) to celebrate the Feast of Pentecost (Acts 2). Not much information can be found about

Babylon during the Middle Ages, but in modern times, small villages have been established within some of the boundaries of the ancient city.

Over one hundred years before the three Hebrew men were put in the fiery furnace (Daniel 3) or Daniel was in the lions' den (Daniel 6), the prophet Isaiah predicted the demise of Babylon. Remember how Sodom and Gomorrah of the Old Testament were destroyed suddenly by fire and burning sulfur coming down from heaven (Genesis 19:24; Luke 17:29)? Isaiah 13:19 suggests that the destruction of Babylon will be like the destruction of Sodom. "And Babylon, the jewel of the kingdoms . . . will be like Sodom and Gomorrah when God overthrew them" (HCSB). This parallels the description of Babylon's demise in Revelation: "Therefore, these plagues will overtake her [the prostitute, Babylon] in a single day. . . . She will be completely consumed by fire, for the Lord God who judges her is mighty" (Revelation 18:8).

Jeremiah, a contemporary to Daniel, also predicted that Babylon would be radically abolished (Jeremiah 50–51). In addition, the Lord also prophesied about Babylon through Jeremiah that "no one will live there again. Everything will be gone; both people and animals will flee" (Jeremiah 50:3, also vv. 39–40). Bedouins and Arabs won't even temporarily camp there. For "there no nomads will pitch their tents, there no shepherds will rest their flocks" (Isaiah 13:20 NIV). The stones or bricks of ancient Babylon have been reused by the surrounding villages for their constructions. Jeremiah predicted concerning Babylon, "Even your stones will never again be used for building" (Jeremiah 51:26).

Can we really say that these prophecies of Babylon will be fulfilled in the future tribulation? The prophecies about Babylon in Isaiah 13 describe Babylon's destruction as taking place in the future day of the Lord. Isaiah used the special phrase for the tribulation: a woman in labor. "Scream in terror, for the day of the LORD has arrived—the time for the almighty to destroy. . . . Pangs of anguish grip them, like those of a woman in labor" (Isaiah 13:6, 8).

Jesus' great Olivet Discourse on the end times also described the tribulation or the day of the Lord in this manner: "All these events [international wars, famines, and earthquakes] are the beginning of birth pains" (Matthew 24:8 HCSB). Isaiah 13:12 predicts, "I will make people scarcer than gold," reminding us of Jesus' prediction, "Unless that time of calamity [the great tribulation] is shortened, not a single person will survive" (Matthew 24:22).

Here is more. Isaiah 13 predicted, "The heavens will be black above them; the stars will give no light. The sun will be dark when it rises, and the moon will provide no light. . . . For I will shake the heavens . . . in the day of his [the Lord's] fierce anger" (vv. 10, 13). In Jesus' Olivet Discourse, he gave us the time of this cosmic event. According to Jesus, the Babylon of Isaiah 13 must be a Babylon that will be in existence during the great tribulation, when Jesus returns to earth. "Immediately after the anguish of those days [after the great tribulation], the sun will be darkened, the moon will give no light, the stars will fall from the sky, and the powers in the heavens will be shaken. . . . And they will see the Son of Man coming on the clouds of heaven with power and great glory" (Matthew 24:29–30).

In 1983, Saddam Hussein (d. 2006), the president of Iraq, began rebuilding the city of Babylon. He spent more than a billion dollars of profits from oil money on the city's reconstruction. Some construction was done on top of the ancient ruins of the city. He attempted to rebuild adjacent to the ancient city's ruins the massive six-hundred-room palace of the ancient Arab and king of Babylon, Nebuchadnezzar. Archaeologists and historians vehemently objected but were powerless.

Hussein also attempted to identify himself with Nebuchadnezzar. The Arab president inscribed his name in the bricks used in his new construction and renovations of the ancient ruins. This was a clear imitation of what Nebuchadnezzar had done in building the city of Babylon. In 2003, Hussein's plans for rebuilding Babylon were thwarted by the invasion of Iraq and the ensuing Iraq War. It is as if Satan were attempting to accomplish the rebuilding of

Babylon before God's foreordained time and to defeat God by distorting the accuracy of the biblical prophecy, making God a liar.

Babylon Controls the World Economy

The rebuilt city of Babylon will control the world's economy as well as have command over the world's anti-God worldview. Just read Revelation 18. When the rebuilt city of Babylon is at its height, the apostle John tells us, "Because of her [Babylon's] desires for extravagant luxury, the merchants of the world have grown rich" (v. 3). Once Babylon is destroyed, all the world's capitalists and kings will mourn for her. "And the kings of the world who committed adultery with her and enjoyed her great luxury will mourn for her as they see the smoke rising from her charred remains. . . . The merchants of the world will weep and mourn for her, for there is no one left to buy their goods" (vv. 9, 11).

How does the city of Babylon control the kingdoms of the world and their economy? Many have suggested that the economy of the world and even of the Antichrist will be totally dependent on whoever controls the world's oil supply. It is common knowledge that the Arab states in the Middle East are rich in oil. About 50 percent of the world's oil reserves are found in the Middle East. Most of the developed countries of the world rely entirely on oil for the activities of everyday life. Oil is also essential to the military strength of the world's political powers.

As far back as Genesis and the beginning of the city of Babylon, the Scriptures testify to Babylon's wealth in oil. When Nimrod and others began to build Babylon, and the tower to reach heaven, Genesis reports: "In this region bricks were used instead of stone, and tar was used for mortar" (Genesis 11:3). Other Bible translations use the word *asphalt* instead of the word *tar*. Either word suggests that oil was common around the city of Babylon right from its beginning. Perhaps Babylon will control the world's oil, and therefore control the world's economy.

Stage #2: The Destruction of Rebuilt Babylon

Isaiah and Jeremiah predict that rebuilt Babylon will be attacked by the Medes, a group of people who come from the north. "Look, I will stir up the Medes against Babylon" (Isaiah 13:17). The Medes were an ancient people who hated the Babylonians. If Babylon is the Babylon of the end times, who are the Medes? The territory of the ancient Medes is today part of northern Iraq, northwestern Iran, and eastern Syria and Turkey. These areas are occupied today by the Kurdish people. Most agree that the Kurds are a people group who are descendants of the Medes. While many Kurds live in Arabic countries, they are not Arabs. They are multilingual, speaking the language of their resident nation (Persian, Arabic, Turkish). They prefer to speak their own Kurdish language. Currently, the Kurds maintain the hope of one day establishing their own nation of Kurdistan. Generally they have been an unwanted people in the countries where they reside.

Saddam Hussein killed thousands of Kurds in 1987–1988, and many more were massacred by Hussein when the Kurds sided with the United States in the Gulf War. Since Hussein mercilessly slaughtered many of the Kurdish women and children, it appears that the Kurds (Medes) of the future may retaliate. Isaiah describes the merciless treatment of Babylon by the Medes. "Anyone [in Babylon] who is captured will be cut down—run through with a sword. Their little children will be dashed to death before their eyes. Their homes will be sacked, and their wives will be raped" (Isaiah 13:15–16).

A second group of armies will join in the attack on Babylon. Some Bible interpreters understand this second army to be a group of nations that rebels against the Antichrist. This makes sense if the Antichrist makes Babylon his capital. We should not suppose that when the world unites around its evil leader, the Beast, all nations will be absolutely loyal.

It is my understanding that this "group of nations" are allies of the Antichrist. Revelation 17 suggests that it is actually the

Antichrist that God will use to destroy Babylon. What irony. The Antichrist destroys his leading city.

> The scarlet beast [the Antichrist] and his ten horns [ten nations in his Revived Roman Empire] all hate the prostitute. They will strip her naked, eat her flesh, and burn her remains with fire. For God has put a plan into their minds, a plan that will carry out his purposes. They will agree to give their authority to the scarlet beast [Antichrist], and so the words of God will be fulfilled.
>
> vv. 16–17

Why does the Antichrist hate the city of Babylon, the prostitute? Because Babylon controls the economy of the Antichrist's empire and therefore controls the Antichrist as well. The Beast has been in control of the whole world politically and religiously, but not economically. He and his ten-nation confederacy will detest the city of Babylon. In his sovereignty, God will put this plan to destroy Babylon into the minds of the Antichrist and his ten kings. Although the Antichrist does not realize it, he will be carrying out God's plan. Jesus once said, "And if Satan is casting out Satan, he is divided and fighting against himself. His own kingdom will not survive" (Matthew 12:26). Although Jesus was talking about casting demons out of people, the principle applies to Satan's role in the destruction of Babylon. His kingdom will not survive.

Similarly to Revelation 17, Jeremiah 50 seems to address this second group of nations that come against Babylon. "For I am raising up an army of great nations from the north. They will join forces to attack Babylon, and she will be captured. . . . Look! A great army is coming from the north. A great nation and many kings are rising against you from far-off lands. . . . They are coming in battle formation, planning to destroy you, Babylon" (vv. 9, 41–42).

In verse 9, Jeremiah says that an "army [singular] of great nations [plural]" will attack Babylon. Although there are many nations, Jeremiah calls them a single "great army" (v. 41). They are a "great nation" (singular), but have "many kings" (v. 41). This appears to be the Antichrist's world empire (singular) and his alliance of ten nations (plural).

God's People Must Leave Babylon

Several warnings are given in Scripture to God's people in future Babylon. The apostle John writes, "Then I heard another voice from heaven shout, 'My people, you must escape from Babylon. Don't take part in her sins and share her punishment'" (Revelation 18:4 CEV). Jeremiah 50–51 also addresses the future destruction of Babylon. These chapters give a similar command. "But now, flee from Babylon! Leave the land of the Babylonians" (50:8). Again, Jeremiah warned, "Come out, my people, flee from Babylon. Save yourselves! Run from the LORD's fierce anger" (51:45).

Jewish believers in Babylon during the time of Daniel never escaped the city when Cyrus, king of the Medo-Persian Empire, conquered Babylon (539 BC). Daniel himself remained in the city and immediately became an administrator in the Persian government. There was almost no bloodshed when Medo-Persia conquered Babylon.

Stage #3: The Initial but Brief Capture of Jerusalem

This gathering of the world's armies at the great plain of Armageddon has two ultimate purposes for the Antichrist: to destroy Jerusalem and the Jews, and to prevent Jesus from taking rulership over the earth. God has a different plan. "For on that day I will begin to destroy all the nations that come against Jerusalem" (Zechariah 12:9). With their false hope of utterly defeating Jerusalem, the worldwide armies march to the Valley of Jehoshaphat (i.e., to the Kidron Valley). This valley surrounds Jerusalem on the east side of the city. The Old Testament prophet Joel delivered this message from the Lord to the nations:

Let the nations be called to arms. Let them march to the valley of Jehoshaphat. There I, the LORD, will sit to pronounce judgment on them all. . . . Swing the sickle, for the harvest is ripe. Come, tread the grapes, for the winepress is full. The storage vats are overflowing with the wickedness of these people. Thousands upon thousands are waiting in the valley of decision. There the day of the LORD will soon arrive. The sun and moon will grow dark, and the stars will no longer shine . . . and the heavens and the earth will shake. But the LORD will be a refuge for his people, a strong fortress for the people of Israel.

Joel 3:12–16

God will greatly energize the Jewish people toward the end of the tribulation at the return of Christ to the earth. At first, great devastation will come on Israel until they acknowledge the sin of rejecting their Messiah. In the Holocaust of World War II, 6 million Jews were killed. According to the prophet Zechariah, in the tribulation, two-thirds of the Jewish people will die, but one-third will live and come to faith in Jesus as Messiah. It is possible that the destruction of this two-thirds may be limited to those who are "in the land" of Israel at the time of the invasion.

"Two-thirds of the people in the land will be cut off and die," says the LORD. "But one-third will be left in the land. I will bring that group through the fire [the tribulation] and make them pure. . . . They will call on my name, and I will answer them. I will say, 'These are my people,' and they will say, 'The LORD is our God.'"

Zechariah 13:8–9

Satan and the Antichrist are radically anti-Semitic, hating all Jews and especially those Jews who accept Jesus as their Messiah. Since the Antichrist will control the political and national powers of the whole world, he will direct all nations to come together to fight against Israel in the day of the Lord. At first, Jerusalem and the Jewish people will be overwhelmed. The initial losses will be great.

> Watch, for the day of the LORD is coming. . . . I will gather all the nations to fight against Jerusalem. The city will be taken, the houses looted, and the women raped. Half the population will be taken into captivity, and the rest will be left among the ruins of the city.
>
> Zechariah 14:1–2

"All the nations" could certainly include the United States, perhaps by that time part of the European coalition of nations directed by the Antichrist. If the rapture takes all believers from the earth, the remaining leaders of the United States and the world will have very few, if anyone, who will support Israel. The nations of the world will be eager to destroy Jerusalem and the Jews.

Zechariah describes the excitement of the nations over destroying Jerusalem as a person longing for a drink of wine (12:2). Once they drink, they become intoxicated. As the nations begin to fulfill their desires against Jerusalem, they become completely unaware that judgment will come on them suddenly from the Lord. In fact, the outcome will soon be reversed and the nations that come against Israel will be destroyed.

Stage #4: The Fighting and Protection of the Remnant at Bozrah

Most of the Jewish people who believe in Jesus as their Messiah are not present in Jerusalem when the city is attacked by the forces of the Antichrist. During the first half of the tribulation, many Jews have come to faith in Jesus through the two mighty prophets (two witnesses) described in Revelation 11:3–12. In chapter 7, we suggested that at the midpoint of the tribulation, these Jewish Christians in Jerusalem will need to flee the city of Jerusalem quickly. Undoubtedly, they will have read or have heard Jesus' instructions in his Olivet Discourse, probably through the two powerful prophets. These Jews will have realized that they must escape for their lives when they see the abomination that causes desolation in the Jerusalem temple (Matthew 24:15–20). Jesus commanded them to run immediately to the mountains.

We also saw in chapter 7 that in John's vision in Revelation 12, the Jewish people are pictured corporately as a woman. John writes, "The woman [Israel] fled into the wilderness, where God had prepared a place to care for her for 1,260 days" (v. 6). Jesus told the Jews living in Jerusalem to flee to the mountains [not the wilderness] when they saw the abomination that causes desolation (Matthew 24:16). Which is it? The wilderness or the mountains? It's both—a wilderness-mountainous location prepared ahead of time by God. In the Old Testament, this location is called Bozrah.

Bozrah is a city in the region called Edom in the Old Testament, a mountainous area in southwestern Jordan today. Archaeological searches have not identified with certainty the precise location of Bozrah. The best suggestion identifies Bozrah with the ruins of a city adjacent to modern Burseira, Jordan, southeast of the Dead Sea. Just six miles (10 km) away to the west sits the abandoned, ancient rock city of Petra. The hidden city of Petra, built by an ancient people called the Nabateans, was not rediscovered in modern times until 1812.

Petra is an unusual but natural basin completely surrounded by towering rocks and cliffs, and is supplied with water by a perpetual stream. Petra is about ninety miles (144 km) southeast of Jerusalem. The only entrance leading into this rock city is a narrow gorge over a mile long and never more than sixteen feet wide. Here's some trivia: This narrow gorge at Petra and the façade of the "temple" (burial site) at the end of the gorge are featured in the 1989 American movie *Indiana Jones and the Last Crusade*. Neither the inner remains of the city nor the actual inside of the "temple" are pictured in the movie.

Several Bible passages speak of a remnant, a surviving group of Jewish people, who will flee to Bozrah during the tribulation. The prophet Micah wrote, "I'll surely gather Jacob—all of you! I'll surely assemble you, those who are left of Israel! I'll put them together like sheep in Bozrah, like a flock in its pen, noisy with people" (2:12 CEB). The name *Bozrah* means "sheep pen." Some versions translate this verse without using the proper name *Bozrah*. For example, the NLT reads, "I will bring you together again like sheep *in a pen* [= Bozrah]." Petra is shaped much like a huge sheep pen formed from rock.

The flight of the Jews to Bozrah will be for their complete provision and protection. As they make their flight, John saw in his vision:

> The dragon tried to drown the woman with a flood of water that flowed from his mouth. But the earth helped her by opening its mouth and swallowing the river that gushed out from the mouth of the dragon. And the dragon was angry at the woman and declared war against the rest of her children—all who keep God's commandments and maintain their testimony for Jesus.
>
> Revelation 12:15–17

The water with which the Dragon (Satan) tried to drown the fleeing Jewish people may be literal—an actual flashflood. But in the Old Testament, a flood of water often symbolizes an army pursuing its enemy (cf. Isaiah 8:7). God protects his remnant by opening the earth and swallowing the army Satan has sent after the Jewish people. This reminds us of how God punished Korah and his followers when they rebelled against Moses (Numbers 16:32).

Satan will apparently counter this defeat by sending more armies against the remnant at Bozrah. The prophet Jeremiah wrote, "I have heard a message from the LORD. . . . 'Form a coalition against Edom, and prepare for battle!' . . . Look! The enemy swoops down like an eagle, spreading his wings over Bozrah. Even the mightiest warriors will be in anguish like a woman in labor" (49:14, 22). The time is the day of the Lord ("anguish like a woman in labor"). The Lord (the "enemy" against this coalition) would swoop down in judgment like an eagle at Bozrah in such a fearful manner that even the "mightiest warriors" will become terrified. God will destroy the armies of the Antichrist and save his people in Bozrah.

Stage #5: The Remnant of Jewish People Come to Faith in Their Messiah

Before the return of Christ to the earth, the remnant of Jewish people on the earth will come to faith in Jesus as their Messiah. For the last two thousand years, the Messiah has been "hidden" from the Jewish people. Blindness has set in on them. They have not been able to "see" that Jesus is their Messiah. The apostle Paul explained it this way: "A partial hardening has come to Israel until the full number of the Gentiles has come in. And in this way all Israel will be saved" (Romans 11:25–26 HCSB). Once God is done with his purposes to bring Gentiles to faith, he will again move among the Jewish people to bring them to faith in Jesus. When God "saves" Israel, it does not mean only their new spiritual birth but also deliverance from their enemies.

The Messiah will not come to the aid of his Jewish people "until they admit their guilt and turn to me [their God and Messiah]. For as soon as trouble comes [the great tribulation], they will earnestly search for me" (Hosea 5:15). Many Jews will turn to their Messiah during the first half of the tribulation. The prophet Hosea specified that Israel's greatest turning point will occur during the last three days before Christ returns to earth.

In the next chapter of Hosea, the Jewish people call to one another,

> Come, let us return to the LORD. For He has torn us, and He will heal us; He has wounded us, and He will bind up our wounds. He will revive us after two days, and on the third day He will raise us up so we can live in His presence. Let us strive to know the LORD. His appearance is as sure as the dawn. He will come to us like the rain, like the spring showers that water the land.
>
> 6:1–3 HCSB

The "third day" may be literal. Just three days before Jesus returns to earth to rescue his Jewish people, the nation of Israel will place their faith in Jesus for eternal life. Since Jesus was resurrected on the third day, the third day may also symbolize the spiritual resurrection of Israel. Jesus will rescue them from their enemies because he will personally appear at his second coming for his Jewish people. His appearance is as sure as the sun rising in the morning and as refreshing as the rain that brings showers in the spring (v. 3).

Stage #6 will be treated in the next chapter.

10

What Is the Second Coming of Christ to the Earth?

Sometimes we think that the first coming of Christ is the most important truth to our Christian faith. This is because at his first coming, Jesus was born of a woman and became fully human. Then after about thirty-three years, he died for our sins as a human substitute and was raised from the dead to prove our sins were fully forgiven. The second coming of Christ is just as essential to our Christian faith. At his second coming to the earth, Jesus will demonstrate his supreme authority to judge the wicked of this world and to reign as king over his creation. He will fully display his glory for all the world to see. He will also severely restrict Satan from working on the earth, climaxing in Satan's final consignment to the eternal lake of fire.

Stage #6: The Second Coming of Christ to the Earth

When? When will Jesus return? At the second coming of Christ to the earth, there will be very clear signs of his return. He himself explained, "So if someone tells you, 'Look, the Messiah is out in the desert,' don't bother to go and look. Or, 'Look, he is hiding here,' don't believe it!" (Matthew 24:26). These statements only make sense if Jesus will come down to the earth, and not stay hidden in the clouds as in the rapture (when only the believers will see him). Jesus' return to earth will be as visible and brilliant as flashes of lightning across the sky: "For as the lightning flashes in the east and shines to the west, so it will be when the Son of Man comes" (v. 27). No one alive will be able to miss his return to the earth. Somehow his glory will be visible from all angles and directions of the globe.

Jesus also gave a very specific time reference for his coming to the earth.

> Immediately after the tribulation of those days: The sun will be darkened, and the moon will not shed its light; the stars will fall from the sky, and the celestial powers will be shaken. Then the sign of the Son of Man will appear in the sky, and then all the peoples of the earth will mourn; and they will see the Son of Man coming on the clouds of heaven with power and great glory.
>
> Matthew 24:29–30 HCSB

Many people who become Christians in the tribulation will quickly understand from Scripture that the "abomination of desolation" in the rebuilt temple in Jerusalem will take place at the midpoint of the seven-year tribulation. When the abomination that causes desolation takes place, there will be exactly three and a half more years, or 1,260 days, before Jesus returns to earth. So "immediately after the tribulation of those days" is a very specific, predictable time.

The "sign of the Son of Man" appearing in the sky (v. 30) will be his divine glory, brilliantly and powerfully breaking through the atmosphere. Everyone will see his radiance, but the Jewish people specifically will be struck with sorrow over his crucifixion, which they had arranged. Remember, Jesus reminded his followers, "No one can take my life from me. I sacrifice it voluntarily"

(John 10:18). From an eternal perspective, the crucifixion of Jesus was not brought about by the human instrumentality of the Jews.

How? How will Jesus return? He will return in mighty power and great glory—unlike his lowly birth in an insignificant Jewish town and his infant care in a manger. In the rapture, Jesus will appear in the sky to catch up the dead in Christ and all true Christians alive at that time. We will see him in the air when we are caught up to be with him forever. The rapture will be an event that happens without warning or distinct signs that give any hint of its arrival. After we are caught up to be with Christ, we will all return with Christ to his Father's house in heaven.

The second coming of Christ to earth will be much different. It is then that his power will be displayed in the destruction of his enemies. The world's armies will be of no threat to Christ, the Warrior and King. Several times Revelation pictures Jesus as completely destroying his enemies at the battle of the great day of God. "From his mouth came a sharp sword to strike down the nations. He will rule them with an iron rod. He will release the fierce wrath of God, the Almighty, like juice flowing from a winepress" (Revelation 19:15). Since the Word of God is like a sharp sword (Hebrews 4:12), this imagery of a sword coming from the mouth of Jesus suggests that he will merely speak, and his enemies will be utterly defeated.

At Jesus' first coming, he rode a donkey (Matthew 21:4–7), a humble animal that carries a heavy load. Jesus, in humility, carried the load of our sins to the cross. At the second coming, he will ride a white horse (Revelation 19:11), symbolic of a righteous, victorious warfare. He also wears many crowns, like the crown a king wears (v. 12), and "He wore a robe stained with blood" (v. 13 HCSB).

What? What does Jesus do when he returns to earth? Once Jesus returns, he will immediately strike down all the nations' armies (19:15). The bodies of the slain enemy warriors will be numerous, and the birds of the air will gorge themselves on the dead bodies (v. 21). An angel calls out to the vultures flying in the sky, "Come!

147

Gather together for the great banquet God has prepared. Come and eat the flesh of kings, generals, and strong warriors; of horses and their riders; and of all humanity, both free and slave, small and great" (vv. 17–18).

In Jesus' victory, he will be accompanied by armies, neither of which will enter into the fight. "The armies of heaven, dressed in the finest of pure white linen, followed him on white horses" (v. 14). The armies (plural) involve all the raptured saints who have been in heaven during the tribulation. They will always be with Christ. They follow him to the earth at his second coming. They participate in his victory, but not in the warfare.

Jesus will also have an army of all the angels with him. "But when the Son of Man comes in his glory, and all the angels with him, then he will sit upon his glorious throne" (Matthew 25:31). All the angels with him? Perhaps heaven itself will be emptied of all these servants of God. What will they do when they arrive on earth? First, Jesus "will send forth His angels with a great trumpet and they will gather together His elect [the Jewish people who have believed in Jesus] from the four winds, from one end of the sky to the other" (Matthew 24:31 NASB).

This is the fulfillment of the prediction of Isaiah 27, the only other passage that mentions a "great trumpet." "Yet the time will come when the LORD will gather them together like handpicked grain. One by one he will gather them. . . . In that day the great trumpet will sound. Many who were dying in exile in Assyria and Egypt will return to Jerusalem to worship the LORD on his holy mountain" (vv. 12–13). These believing Jews will return to Jerusalem for the one-thousand-year reign of Christ on earth.

There are two gatherings of the Jewish people prophesied in the Old Testament: one in unbelief in the Messiah and one in belief. The gathering of the Jewish people in unbelief took place in 1948 and the years that followed. The second gathering of Israel will be at the second coming of Jesus to earth. "In that day the Lord will reach out his hand a second time to bring back the remnant of his people. . . . He will gather the scattered people of Judah from the ends of the earth" (Isaiah 11:11–12). This is a worldwide gathering of faithful Jews.

Finally, when Jesus returns to earth, he must deal with the leaders of this worldwide rebellion, the Antichrist, the False Prophet, and Satan. First, Jesus will capture the Beast, or Antichrist. He will also seize the False Prophet "who did mighty miracles on behalf of the beast—miracles that deceived all who had accepted the mark of the beast and who worshiped his statue. Both the beast and his false prophet were thrown alive into the fiery lake of burning sulfur" (Revelation 19:20). The lake of fire is the final place of punishment for the wicked. In other places, the Bible calls this place *hell*.

The Beast and the False Prophet are the very first two who are cast into the lake of fire. In fact, no one is in the lake of fire yet. All the dead who have refused to believe in the one true God (Old Testament) or Jesus his Son (New Testament) are confined to a temporary place of painful judgment (Luke 16:22–24) until they are given their final sentencing at the great white throne judgment.

Where? The Lord Jesus will return to earth shortly after Jerusalem has been violently besieged. Where does Jesus step down on the surface of the earth? Many Bible teachers believe Jesus first steps onto the Mount of Olives just east of the city of Jerusalem. Then he destroys the armies of the Antichrist who have plundered Jerusalem. They draw this conclusion from Zechariah 14:4, "On that day his feet will stand on the Mount of Olives, east of Jerusalem."

Other Bible teachers suggest that Jesus will first come to Bozrah to rescue the remnant of Israel. Isaiah 63 seems to suggest that the Messiah comes to Bozrah first, then proceeds to Jerusalem. Isaiah 63 begins with the prophet (or an imaginary watchman), apparently in Jerusalem, asking for the identity of the warrior coming from Bozrah. The warrior has the apparel of a king, but his robe is stained with blood from combat.

> Who is this who comes from Edom, from the city of Bozrah, with his clothing stained red? Who is this in royal robes, marching in his great strength? "It is I, the LORD [Jesus the Messiah], announcing

your salvation! It is I, the LORD, who has the power to save! 'Why are your clothes so red, as if you have been treading out grapes?' I have been treading the winepress alone; no one was there to help me. In my anger I have trampled my enemies as if they were grapes. . . . Their blood has stained my clothes. For the time has come for me to avenge my [Jewish] people, to ransom them from their oppressors. . . . I crushed the nations in my anger."

vv. 1–4, 6

The book of Revelation uses much of the same imagery in its description of Jesus' second coming (Revelation 14:19–20; 19:13). Isaiah 63 suggests that Jesus defeats his enemies who have attacked Bozrah and the remnant of Jewish people there. Then he marches toward Jerusalem to finish his defeat of the armies of the Antichrist in the Kidron Valley. Zechariah 12:7 says, "The LORD will give victory to the rest of Judah [i.e., those in Bozrah] first, before Jerusalem."

God first strikes the Antichrist's worldwide armies and supplies. "'On that day,' says the LORD, 'I will cause every horse to panic and every rider to lose his nerve. I will watch over the people of Judah, but I will blind all the horses of their enemies'" (Zechariah 12:4). Then God will supernaturally empower the Jewish people in Jerusalem in their fight against the world's armies (vv. 5–6). They will so quickly destroy their enemies that it will be "like a burning torch among sheaves of grain."

"On that day the LORD will defend the people of Jerusalem; the weakest among them will be as mighty as King David! . . . For on that day I will begin to destroy all the nations that come against Jerusalem" (Zechariah 12:8–9). Without any previous military training, the average Israeli will fight like the mighty warrior that King David was.

It is at this time that the Lord will "pour out a spirit of grace and prayer on the family of David and on the people of Jerusalem" (Zechariah 12:10). They will look on the Messiah and mourn bitterly over the fact that they, as his chosen people, have rejected him for two thousand years.

As Jesus reaches Jerusalem, he takes his victory stand on the Mount of Olives. "Then the LORD will go out to fight against those nations, as he has fought in times past. On that day his feet will stand on the Mount of Olives, east of Jerusalem. And the Mount of Olives will split apart, making a wide valley running from east to west. Half the mountain will move toward the north and half toward the south. You will flee through this valley" (Zechariah 14:3–5). A believing remnant among the Jews will flee from Jerusalem to safety along this valley.

Why will Jesus stand on the Mount of Olives at the second coming to earth? It was from the Mount of Olives that Jesus ascended into heaven (Acts 1:11–12). In Acts 1:3, we read, "During the forty days after he suffered and died, he appeared to the apostles from time to time. . . . And he talked to them about the Kingdom of God." What was this kingdom Jesus referred to? It was the restoration of the kingdom promised to Israel in the Old Testament over which the Messiah would be king. That's why the apostles kept asking Jesus, "Lord, has the time come for you to free Israel and restore our kingdom?" (Acts 1:6). The question wasn't, "*Will* you restore our kingdom?" but "Has the time come for you to restore our kingdom?" They knew that Jesus wouldn't have contradicted or annulled the Old Testament promises to restore Israel's kingdom.

Jesus replied to the apostles, "The Father alone has the authority to set those dates and times, and they are not for you to know" (Acts 1:7). In Jesus' teachings and in the apostle Paul's writings, the time that God will restore the kingdom to Israel will be at the end of the tribulation—and no one can know the day or hour when the tribulation will begin (Matthew 24:36). It will come like a thief—without warning. After Jesus promised that the Holy Spirit would soon come to give them power, "he was taken up into a cloud while they were watching, and they could no longer see him" (Acts 1:9). Two angels appeared and exclaimed, "Why are you standing here staring into heaven? Jesus has been taken from you into heaven, but someday he will return from heaven in the same way you saw him go!" (v. 11). Jesus was taken to heaven visibly and physically. Jesus' ascension was from the Mount of Olives, so he will return visibly, physically to the Mount of Olives. He ascended to glory; he will descend in glory.

This kingdom that Jesus spoke about while he was with the apostles is the subject of chapter 11 of this book.

The Resurrection of the Dead

Believers from the New Testament Era. Most people usually picture a single event in which everyone who has ever lived will be resurrected and brought before God and Jesus for final judgment. This is not quite the case. Instead, there are several different times in which people will be resurrected and judged. Every true Christian of the church age, since the day of Pentecost in Acts 2 up to the rapture, is resurrected at once. Paul gave an order or sequence to the resurrection at the rapture. "First, the believers who have died will rise from their graves. Then, together with them, we who are still alive and remain on the earth will be caught up in the clouds to meet the Lord in the air" (1 Thessalonians 4:16–17). Even though these resurrections take place at basically the same moment, there is a sequence. The dead believers will precede the living.

Paul wrote to the Corinthian church, adding additional elements to the sequence: "But there is an order to this resurrection: Christ was raised as the first of the harvest; then all who belong to Christ will be raised when he comes back" (1 Corinthians 15:23). All resurrections will follow Christ's resurrection. That means that when Moses and Elijah appeared with Jesus on the Mount of Transfiguration (Matthew 17:1–8), these two Old Testament patriarchs were not in their final, resurrected bodies. In the case of Lazarus, whom Jesus raised from the dead after four days in the grave (John 11), he came back to life in a physical body that would die again.

Believers from the Old Testament Era. After the rapture, the next resurrection will take place at the end of the tribulation when Jesus comes back to earth. It is then that the resurrection of Old Testament believers will take place. They are the ones who have trusted in the one true God as he was revealed at that time. In other words, today we must believe that Jesus is the Messiah. In the Old Testament times, they believed in a coming Messiah, but certainly didn't need to know his name was Jesus. In fact, they couldn't have known that. These Old Testament believers are people like Abraham, Sarah, Moses, Ruth, King David, the prophets, and many, many more—even many Jewish people who are never named in the Bible. They also include Gentiles like Rahab, Ruth, and the citizens of Nineveh (Jonah 3).

Daniel 12 gives us the time for this resurrection. An angel (or the Messiah) explained to Daniel that Michael, the archangel, would rise up in the future tribulation to protect the Jewish people. When he rises up, "there will be a time of anguish greater than any since nations first came into existence" (Daniel 12:1). Jesus also referred to this time of anguish like no other when he said, "For at that time there will be great tribulation, the kind that hasn't taken place from the beginning of the world until now and never will again!" (Matthew 24:21 HCSB). This is, of course, the great tribulation that precedes the coming of Christ to the earth.

The angel told Daniel, "But at that time [at the end of the great tribulation] every one of your people whose name is written in the book will be rescued. Many of those whose bodies lie dead and buried will rise up, some to everlasting life and some to shame and everlasting disgrace" (Daniel 12:1–2). Although there are several different times for people to be resurrected, there are basically only two kinds of resurrection: a resurrection to life and a resurrection to death and suffering. Daniel 12:2 is the clearest verse in the Old Testament about a future resurrection.

How can there be a resurrection to death? Revelation 20 actually calls the resurrection to eternal punishment a "second death." The first death is physical death; the second death is eternal death. The Bible doesn't use the term *life* for the experience of those who reject the gospel of Jesus Christ. Since life is the experience of a joyful and blessed relationship with the living God, it cannot be used of the experience of those who reject the truth of God. Unbelievers do not experience an afterlife but an "after death."

Believers Who Have Died During the Tribulation. It only makes sense that those who have died during the tribulation will have to be resurrected sometime after the tribulation is completed. In other words, tribulation believers will be resurrected at basically the same time as Old Testament believers. The book of Revelation confirms this. Note the order of events in Revelation 19:21—20:1–6. Revelation 19:21 is the last verse in that chapter, so read right through the chapter division. (By the way, chapter divisions were created in Bibles in the early thirteenth century; verse divisions and numbering were created in the mid-sixteenth century.)

1. Jesus destroys his enemies in the battle of the great day of God (Armageddon). "Their entire army was killed by the sharp sword that came from the mouth of the one riding the white horse" (Revelation 19:21).

2. Satan is completely restricted and incapacitated for the one-thousand-year reign of Jesus on earth (Revelation 20:1–3).

3. Next, John "saw the souls of those who had been beheaded for their testimony about Jesus. . . . They had not worshiped the beast or his statue, nor accepted his mark on their foreheads or their hands. They all came to life again [were resurrected], and they reigned with Christ for a thousand years. This is the first resurrection" (20:4–5).

Since these faithful followers of Christ didn't take the mark of the Beast—and the mark of the Beast is enforced during the entire second half of the tribulation—they are resurrected when the tribulation comes to an end.

Resurrections

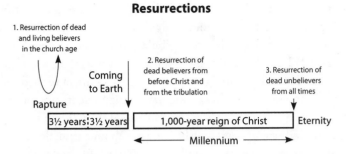

Just as Daniel mentioned the resurrection to eternal life first in his order of two resurrections, so does John. Believers from the tribulation are part of "the first resurrection" (Revelation 20:5). John adds a parenthetical remark in verse 5 that explains when all unbelievers are resurrected: "(The rest of the dead did not come to life until the thousand years were ended)" (NIV). The "rest of the dead" refers to all unbelievers from all eras of life on earth. This seems evident from the apostle's next comment. "Blessed and holy are those who share in the first resurrection. For them the second death holds no power, but they will be priests of God and of Christ and will reign with him a thousand years" (Revelation 20:6). The rest of the dead will experience the "second death." The judgment of unbelievers will be discussed in chapter 12 of this book.

Seventy-Five Days Before the Millennium

Shortly after the revelation to Daniel of the future resurrection, two more angelic figures joined the original heavenly being who was speaking to Daniel. Daniel listened in as one of the two angels asked the first heavenly being, "How long will it be until these shocking events are over?" (Daniel 12:5). In other words, how long will there be "a time of anguish greater than any since nations first came into existence"? (v. 1). The leading angel answered, "It will go on for a time, times, and half a time. When the shattering of the holy people [the Jewish people] has finally come to an end, all these things will have happened" (v. 7). Once again, the time designation refers to three and a half years, 1,260 days, or forty-two months. At the end of the great tribulation, the Jewish people will be greatly humbled and come to faith in Jesus as their Messiah.

Daniel asked for further clarification. The angel replied that those who are wise will gain understanding by searching out the meanings of the prophecies. He also added this: "From the time that the daily sacrifice is abolished and the abomination that causes desolation is set up, there will be 1,290 days. Blessed is the one who waits for and reaches the end of the 1,335 days. As for you, go your way till the end. You will rest, and then at the end of the days you will rise to receive your allotted inheritance" (Daniel 12:11–13 NIV). The observant reader can see that these figures add several days to the original 1,260 days of the great tribulation: 1,260 + 30 = 1,290 days, and 1,290 + 45 = 1,335 days. A total of seventy-five days are added to the great tribulation of 1,260 days.

Why are these seventy-five days added to the three and a half years of the great tribulation? No Scripture clarifies this directly, but a few hints are given. Daniel 12:11 implies that the 1,290 days focus on the abomination that causes desolation. Daniel 9 predicts that this sacrilegious object (a statue or image of the Antichrist; Mark 13:14; Revelation 13:14–15) will be set up in the temple in Jerusalem at the midpoint of the Seventieth Week of Daniel. When Jesus sets up his kingdom to begin his one-thousand-year reign, this image will certainly be removed or destroyed. With many other activities to bring in Christ's kingdom, perhaps the statue of the Antichrist will finally be destroyed after thirty days.

Another hint is found in the description of the extra forty-five days (or seventy-five days total). Daniel 12:12 states, "Blessed is the one who waits for and reaches the end of the 1,335 days" (NIV). This blessing seems to be the blessing for those believers who are still alive at the end of the great tribulation. I will discuss this in the next chapter. Here is a brief list of other things that may take place during this seventy-five day interval between Christ's coming to earth and the beginning of his one-thousnd-year reign.

1. The Antichrist and False Prophet will be thrown into the lake of fire (Revelation 19:20).

2. Satan will be bound and restrained in the abyss (Revelation 20:1–3). Demons will be prevented from doing their evil as well. "I will also do away with their prophets [i.e., Israel's false prophets] and those evil spirits that control them" (Zechariah 13:2 CEV).

3. The construction of the fourth Jerusalem temple will take place (Ezekiel 40–43).

4. The bodies of those who were killed in the war of the great day of God (Armageddon) will need to be removed and buried.

5. The administration of the kingdom will be organized, such as who will rule with Christ, where they will rule, and what will be their responsibilities.

6. The wedding feast of the Lamb will take place (Revelation 19:7–9).

7. The judgment of the still-living Gentiles will determine which Gentiles will be permitted to enter the kingdom (Matthew 25:31–46).

Several of these events will be described in the next chapter.

11

What Is the Millennium?

The *Hallelujah Chorus*, from Handel's *Messiah*, is one of the most well-known pieces of music ever written. It was composed in 1741 by a committed Christian, Georg Friedrich Handel. In many parts of the Western world, audiences stand during the *Hallelujah Chorus*. The practice is said to have developed when King George II was so moved by the music when he heard it that he stood to his feet and required that his subjects do the same.

The text of the *Messiah* was composed by a friend of Handel who pulled together fragments of Scripture relating to the whole life of Jesus. The *Hallelujah Chorus* describes the second coming of Christ to the earth. The words are taken from the King James Version of Revelation 19:6: "Alleluia: for the Lord God omnipotent reigneth" and 11:15: "The kingdoms of this world are become the kingdoms of our Lord, and of his Christ; and he shall reign for ever and ever," and Revelation 19:16: "KING OF KINGS, AND LORD OF LORDS."

What does *millennium* mean? When Jesus comes to earth, he will set up his kingdom on earth as the first stage of his rule over the world and over eternity. This first stage is called the "millennium."

Millennium comes from two Latin words meaning "one thousand years." We are currently living in the third millennium AD, the third one-thousand-year period since the birth of Christ. The word *millennium* doesn't actually appear in the Bible, but a period of one thousand years is mentioned six times in Revelation 20. So many Christians refer to this one thousand years as the millennium.

Christians throughout history have had different views on what this one thousand years involves. Many take the one thousand years as symbolic of an indefinite period of time, usually as a description of the whole church age. Within this group, some understand the millennium to be an unseen spiritual kingdom. Christ rules this present spiritual kingdom either on earth in and through the hearts of true Christians and the Christian church, or in heaven along with all believers who have died.

There is certainly an unseen kingdom of God in the world. God's kingdom, his unseen rule over the world and its rulers, has always existed, even in Old Testament times. King Nebuchadnezzar, the powerful king of the Babylonian Empire during the time of Daniel, ultimately acknowledged God's universal kingdom rule over the world: "His kingdom will last forever, his rule through all generations" (Daniel 4:3). This kingdom of God existed in the time of Nebuchadnezzar. It involved God's sovereign power over all earthly kings. Daniel also recognized this kingdom of God. He gave praise to God: "He controls the course of world events; he removes kings and sets up other kings" (Daniel 2:21). But this kingdom is not quite the same as the future rule of Jesus on earth for one thousand years.

It is at the end of the great tribulation when an angel blows the seventh trumpet and announces, "The kingdom of the world has become the kingdom of our Lord and his Christ, and he will rule forever and always" (Revelation 11:15 CEB). The verse teaches that Jesus' kingdom does not arrive until the end of all the earthly kingdoms ruled by people. Jesus' kingdom replaces the kingdom of the world. Most versions read, "the kingdom [singular] of the world," rather than the "kingdoms [plural] of this world" (found in the KJV, NKJV). When Jesus returns to earth, the Antichrist will

160

be ruling the world. Only one kingdom will be in existence when Jesus sets up his kingdom in the millennium. The Antichrist will have unwittingly prepared for the kingdom of God.

Other Christians, including myself, consider this one thousand years to be a future kingdom and to involve precisely one thousand years. In my understanding, most numbers with time in Revelation are actual periods of time. We saw that the forty-two months in Revelation 11:2 helped identify the 1,260 days mentioned in 11:3. This combination suggests the time designations are normal and factual, not symbolic. Also, Revelation 5:10 states, "And you have caused them to become a Kingdom of priests for our God. And they will reign on the earth." The last phrase states directly that people—those who have trusted Christ—will reign as kings on the earth, not primarily in heaven.

Christ's future kingdom won't be only spiritual. Christians (and non-Christians as well) sometimes have wrong thinking about what *spiritual* means. We are under the impression that whatever is spiritual must *not* also be physical. God never identifies the physical as sinful by itself. He created the first human couple as physical beings and identified the creation of the heavens and the earth as good. They were created without sin and without a curse. In his resurrection, Jesus had a physical body—and will always have a physical body, even in all of eternity. During his forty days on earth after his physical resurrection, Jesus ate, walked, talked, and was visible to others, such as his disciples, several women, and more than five hundred followers at one time (1 Corinthians 15:6). Thomas was the apostle who doubted Jesus' resurrection the most. He insisted that he would not believe Jesus was raised from the dead until he saw and felt the pierce marks in Jesus' hands and side that he received at his crucifixion. Thomas did touch Jesus' hands and side because his resurrected body was a physical body. What is spiritual can also be physical.

The millennium is Christ's reign on the physical earth for one thousand years. At the beginning of the millennium, John states that Jesus will dramatically prevent Satan from all activity on the earth. After the one thousand years, "he [Satan] must be released for *a little while*" (Revelation 20:3). The apostle John knows how to speak of an indefinite period of time if he wants to. Why take the one thousand years to be symbolic of an indefinite period of time?

I understand Revelation 20 to describe the restored kingdom of Israel mentioned in Acts 1, as we discussed in the last chapter. It is true that the exact length of this kingdom or millennium (the one thousand years) is only mentioned in Revelation 20. But the kingdom itself is a major theme throughout the Old Testament and Jesus' teachings. Recall our discussion of Daniel 2, where the stone cut out of a mountain struck the statue (chapter 8). "During the reigns of those [ten future] kings, the God of heaven will set up a kingdom that will never be destroyed or conquered. It will crush all these kingdoms into nothingness, and it will stand forever" (Daniel 2:44).

This is describing the millennium. God's kingdom in Daniel 2 is physical like other earthly kingdoms. The "stone cut out of the mountain without human hands" (the Messiah and his kingdom) does not coexist with other earthly kingdoms. It replaces all other earthly kingdoms. It is not as though the human kingdoms are physical and political, and in contrast the messianic kingdom is heavenly and spiritual. The messianic kingdom (the kingdom of God) is a political kingdom because Jesus will rule on the earth as a sovereign—as a king, as a monarch. It's not a democracy; it's a theocracy—a rulership by God on earth. Revelation 19:15 quotes the Old Testament to reflect Jesus' strong leadership: "He will rule them with an iron rod." But this truth must be kept in mind: At the end of the millennium, things will change because the millennium is only the first stage of God's eternal kingdom, a kingdom that will extend beyond the millennium.

Why a Millennium?

What is the purpose of the millennium? First, God needs to show the whole world that the problems they have been facing on earth are the result of sin in the human heart, and nothing else. Ever since creation, humans have blamed God for their problems, directly or indirectly. The people of the world believe that they are basically good. They vehemently deny that evil deep in the human heart is the primary cause of wars, crimes, tragedies, and of death itself. Humans as a whole also refuse to believe that the first step toward the solution of these problems is found in personal faith in Jesus Christ as Savior and Lord. God will institute a perfect environment during this time in which people will live but will have the same sinful hearts that have characterized all people since the original sin of Adam and Eve. In this way, the problems of the world will be seen more clearly to result from human rebellion against God.

Second, God made numerous promises to Israel in the covenants he confirmed in the Old Testament. Many parts of these promises have never yet been fulfilled. God made a one-way covenant with Abraham. God alone was responsible to fulfill the covenant that would place Abraham's descendants in the land of Israel permanently (Genesis 17:8). In the covenant that God made with King David, the Lord said, "I will raise up one of your descendants, your own offspring, and I will make his kingdom strong. . . . And I will secure his royal throne forever. . . . Your house and your kingdom will continue before me for all time, and your throne will be secure forever" (2 Samuel 7:12–13, 16). The angel Gabriel repeated this promise to Mary at Jesus' birth: "The Lord God will give him [Jesus] the throne of his ancestor David. And he will reign over Israel forever; his Kingdom will never end!" (Luke 1:32–33). God will begin his fulfillment of these promises in the millennial kingdom.

Who Will Go into the Millennium?

At his second coming to earth, Jesus will destroy all of his enemies who have gathered at Armageddon to fight against him. Then the Lord will send out his angels to gather the elect Jewish people who have been scattered, many hiding in various places around the world. There will also be many Gentiles who have come to faith and are in various locations around the world. They may have been in hiding and have somehow escaped the Antichrist's universal command to worship him and take the mark of the Beast. These Gentile believers have helped the Jewish believers who were being sought out by the Antichrist's "Gestapo." After Christ steps onto the Mount of Olives and pronounces his victory, these Gentiles will be gathered together to be judged by Christ. Therefore, this judgment is on earth. Those found to have true Christian faith will enter Christ's messianic kingdom, the millennium.

As I suggested earlier, most, if not all, living Jews will come to faith in their true Messiah near the end of the tribulation. Isaiah 60:21 addresses Israel regarding the future kingdom: "All your people will be righteous. They will possess their land forever, for I will plant them there with my own hands in order to bring myself glory." Ezekiel 20:34, 38 states, "And in anger [the tribulation] I will reach out with my strong hand and powerful arm, and I will bring you back from the lands where you are scattered. . . . I will purge you of all those who rebel and revolt against me. I will bring them out of the countries where they are in exile, but they will never enter the land of Israel." Only the Jewish people who have come to faith in the Messiah Jesus will enter the kingdom.

In the Olivet Discourse, Jesus taught a parable about the judgment of Gentiles he called "sheep" and "goats" (Matthew 25:31–46). This judgment also takes place at Jesus' second coming to earth: "But when the Son of Man comes in his glory, and all the angels with him, then he will sit upon his glorious throne." This is the throne promised in the Davidic covenant. Since Jesus takes his seat as King on a throne, this is the beginning of his kingdom. Jesus continues, "All the nations will be gathered in his [the Son of Man's] presence, and he will separate the people as a shepherd separates the sheep from the goats" (Matthew 25:31–32). The original Greek word for *nations* in this verse also means "Gentiles." This judgment is a judgment of individual people, not a judgment of the various countries of the world. Since it is a judgment of Gentiles, it is limited to non-Jewish individuals.

Recall that Jesus prophesied, "And the Good News about the Kingdom will be preached throughout the whole world, so that all nations [i.e., all Gentiles] will hear it; and then the end will come" (Matthew 24:14). By the end of the tribulation, everyone in the world will have heard that message about Jesus, about his coming kingdom, and about his power to deliver us from sin. No one in the world will have an excuse for not accepting Christ as their personal Savior.

In Jesus' parable, he tells the sheep (the ones called "righteous," 25:37) that they will inherit the kingdom because when he was hungry, sick, or in prison, they met his desperate needs. The sheep are startled. When had they ever helped Jesus when he was hungry, in prison, or in some other desperate need? Jesus answered, "When you did it to one of the least of these my brothers and sisters, you were doing it to me!" (25:40). The Lord explains to the goats, in a similar manner, that they never met his needs when he was thirsty, naked, sick, or in prison. They too were shocked. How was it that they had refused to serve Jesus in this way? Jesus responded, "When you refused to help the least of these my brothers and sisters, you were refusing to help me" (v. 45). Then he pronounces his judgment: The goats "will go away into eternal punishment, but the righteous [the sheep] will go into eternal life" (v. 46).

Jesus' "brothers and sisters" are obviously a separate group from the sheep and the goats. The sheep didn't help other sheep or goats. They helped Jesus in disguise. In other words, the "brothers and sisters" are not Gentiles like the sheep or goats but faithful Jews like their Savior. Paul referred to his fellow Jews this way: "My heart is filled with bitter sorrow . . . for my people, my Jewish brothers and sisters" (Romans 9:2–3).

During the second half of the tribulation, the Beast will attempt to eliminate all Jewish people throughout the world. The mark of the Beast and the worship of the Antichrist will be extensively enforced worldwide. No one will be able to buy or sell anything without the mark of the Beast. Since the 144,000 are sealed by God (Revelation 7:4–8), these evangelists will be one Jewish group that will not take the mark of the Beast. They may have difficulty supplying for themselves the necessities of life. Those Gentiles who help them will show that they are among the sheep of Jesus' parable.

There may be other Jews in a similar needy situation. Who will help these believing Jews? Anyone who would risk helping these Jews would further endanger themselves by sharing scarce food or limited clothing, which will be very difficult to get without the mark of the Beast. By their life-threatening sacrifice, the sheep will demonstrate that they have true faith in Jesus. On the other hand, any Gentile who has received the mark of the Beast will certainly not help such Jews. That Gentile person's heart is hardened; they will never believe in Jesus (Revelation 14:9–10).

Entering the Millennium

In the parable of the sheep and goats, the sheep receive eternal life. No physical resurrection is mentioned in the parable. Therefore, since the sheep go into the kingdom, they must go into the kingdom with natural, earthly bodies. That also means that all the people who enter this future kingdom will be Christians. Yet they will still have a sinful influence or a sinful nature as do all Christian today. And like Christians today, they will ultimately die physically even though they have eternal life. People in the millennium will also have the privilege of marriage and the ability to have children just as God originally intended for people. As children are born, they will need to believe the gospel of the Lord Jesus in order to gain eternal life, similar to the present age. How do we know all this is true?

In eternity, there will be no death. Death will be abolished. But Bible passages that speak about the millennial kingdom indicate that people will die during the one thousand years. "No longer will babies die when only a few days old. No longer will adults die before they have lived a full life. No longer will people be considered old at one hundred! Only the cursed will die that young!" (Isaiah 65:20).

This passage suggests that there will be no infant mortality in the kingdom (no abortions either). The length of life will be greatly extended. The current highest average age of death in the world is approximately seventy-eight to eighty. But in the millennial kingdom, anyone who dies at age one hundred will seem like someone in our culture who dies in their teens—far too young to die. It is also possible that Isaiah 65:20 means that in the kingdom, a person will have only *until* the age of one hundred to come to faith in Jesus. If they don't come to faith by age one hundred, they will be put to death because they are under God's curse.

Characteristics of the Millennial Kingdom

Universal Knowledge of Jesus and God. The knowledge of the Lord will be available to everyone in the world. No one will be without the message of Jesus or the understanding of the need for faith in Christ, "for the earth shall be full of the knowledge of the LORD as the waters cover the sea" (Isaiah 11:9 ESV). Jesus will be personally present in Jerusalem (Zechariah 8:3, 22) and will teach all who come. "People from many nations will come and say, 'Come, let us go up to the mountain of the LORD [Jerusalem], to the house of Jacob's God [the temple]. There he will teach us his ways, and we will walk in his paths'" (Isaiah 2:3). Despite the widespread knowledge of God, some children will grow up and refuse to believe in Jesus for salvation.

No Crime or Toilsome Work. Work in the millennium will be much more productive and less tedious. The weeds or difficulties of work brought on by sin in the garden of Eden will cease (Genesis 3). "In those days people will live in the houses they build and eat the fruit of their own vineyards. Unlike the past, invaders will not take their houses and confiscate their vineyards. For my people will live as long as trees, and my chosen ones will have time to enjoy their hard-won gains. They will not work in vain, and their children will not be doomed to misfortune" (Isaiah 65:21–23).

Increased Agricultural Productivity. Every wilderness will be turned into highly productive farmland or beautiful, flowering grasslands. "Even the wilderness and desert will be glad in those days. The wasteland will rejoice and blossom with spring crocuses" (Isaiah 35:1). "'The time will come,' says the LORD, 'when the grain and grapes will grow faster than they can be harvested'" (Amos 9:13).

Justice and Righteousness. According to the prophet Isaiah, the Messiah, called the "Branch" or shoot from King David's family, will be so directed by the Spirit of God that he will rule with complete justice and righteousness (Isaiah 11:1–4). "He will give justice to the poor and make fair decisions for the exploited." All outward evil, crime, prejudice, and mistreatment of every sort will be put down quickly. "He will wear righteousness like a belt and truth like an undergarment" (Isaiah 11:5).

A Tamed Animal World. "In that day the wolf and the lamb will live together; the leopard will lie down with the baby goat. The calf and the yearling will be safe with the lion, and a little child will lead them all. . . . Yes, a little child will put its hand in a nest of deadly snakes without harm. Nothing will hurt or destroy in all my holy mountain" (Isaiah 11:6, 8–9). All animals will return to God's original design for them to be plant eaters rather than meat eaters (Genesis 1:30).

Physical Disabilities Will Be Eliminated. "Say to those with fearful hearts, 'Be strong, and do not fear, for your God is coming to destroy your enemies. He is coming to save you.' And when he comes, he will open the eyes of the blind and unplug the ears of the deaf. The lame will leap like a deer, and those who cannot speak will sing for joy!" (Isaiah 35:4–6).

Universal Worship. No other religions and no atheists will exist in the millennium, at least in any outward expression. "And the LORD will be king over all the earth. On that day there will be one

LORD—his name alone will be worshiped" (Zechariah 14:9). Also, in the millennium, the topography of Jerusalem will change. "In the last days, the mountain of the LORD's house will be the highest of all—the most important place on earth. It will be raised above the other hills, and people from all over the world will stream there to worship" (Isaiah 2:2). One reason for this is that "the LORD's [Jesus'] teaching will go out from Zion; his word will go out from Jerusalem" (v. 3).

Universal Peace. There will be no wars anywhere on the earth, for "the LORD will mediate between nations and will settle international disputes. They will hammer their swords into plowshares and their spears into pruning hooks. Nation will no longer fight against nation, nor train for war anymore" (v. 4).

With all of these blessings on the earth, there will be no welfare, no unemployment, no hospitals, no unresolved or unpunished crimes, and complete peace worldwide—at least until the very end of the millennium.

Rebellion at the End of the Millennium

At the very end of the millennium, Satan will be released from the abyss to lead a final rebellion on earth. This will be his last and final attempt to defeat God and Christ—his last stand. "When the thousand years come to an end, Satan will be let out of his prison. He will go out to deceive the nations—called Gog and Magog—in every corner of the earth. He will gather them together for battle—a mighty army, as numberless as sand along the seashore" (Revelation 20:7–8).

Gog and Magog? We've seen those names before. Here in Revelation, they may be used to remind us of the battle pictured in Ezekiel 38–39 (see chapter 8). In this way, they are acting as figurative names of the perpetual enemies of the people of God. Deceived by Satan, the armies of Gog and Magog "surrounded God's people and the beloved city. But fire from heaven came down on the attacking armies and consumed them. Then the devil, who had deceived them, was thrown into the fiery lake of burning sulfur, joining the beast and the false prophet. There they will be tormented day and night forever and ever" (Revelation 20:9–10). Satan is the third one to be cast into the lake of fire. Others will be thrown into the lake of fire when God judges all unbelievers and eternity begins.

12

What Is the Final Judgment, and the New Heaven and New Earth?

Everything that's new and pleasing in eternity will be experienced only by those who are rightly related to God and Jesus. The beginning of eternity cannot take place without the judgment and exclusion of those who have refused to believe in Christ. Sinful thoughts and evil practices cannot be part of God's amazing plan for his people in eternity. Eternity will begin with the great white throne judgment described in Revelation 20.

Some Christians understand the Bible to describe one general judgment in which God determines the eternal destiny of all individuals. This is not quite true. One's eternal destiny is already determined in this life. Jesus said, "Whoever hears my word and believes him who sent me has eternal life. He does not come into judgment" (John 5:24 ESV). The person who has believed in Christ "*has* eternal life," not "will get eternal life one day in the future."

To understand this further, we must turn to the teachings of Jesus. "There is no judgment against anyone who believes in him [i.e., in the Son]. But anyone who does not believe in him has already been judged for not believing in God's one and only Son" (John 3:18). The one who does not believe in Christ is judged already—in this life. The final, future judgment for those who do not believe in Christ is not precisely to determine their eternal destiny. According to Jesus, that is decided on earth. The final judgment of unbelievers, called the great white throne judgment, will prove that the unbeliever is totally deserving of an eternity in hell.

When a genuine Christian dies, he or she goes immediately into the presence of the Savior. Paul said, "We would rather be away from these earthly bodies, for then we will be at home with the Lord" (2 Corinthians 5:8). If I have trusted in the Lord for the forgiveness of my sins, I will immediately go into the personal presence of the Lord at the moment of death. Will God make any mistakes? Could I be mistakenly put in a place of torment? Unthinkable! Similarly, what happens to those who have refused to believe in Christ for eternal life at the time of death? Will Jesus allow such a person into his presence in heaven when he dies? Of course not. Jesus or God the Father will not mistakenly bring an unbeliever into their presence at death. Our eternal destiny is fixed by the decision that we make in this life regarding Jesus.

Unbelievers will immediately go into a temporary place of punishment called "Hades" or "hell" in the Bible. This is similar to how a criminal, after being apprehended, is sent immediately to jail where he waits for his final sentence to a state or federal prison. No one has been assigned yet to the lake of fire, the final place of punishment. The first one to be cast into the lake of fire is the Antichrist at the coming of Jesus to the earth.

Everyone who dies knows at that very moment exactly where they will be for eternity. There is really no need for Christ and the Father to bring all people together in eternity or in heaven to determine their final destiny. This means that there will not be one final gathering of all people to determine their ultimate destiny. That is already decided on earth.

The Judgment Seat of Christ (or of God)

The Participants at the Judgment Seat of Christ. The judgment for all believers who have lived during the church age is called the judgment seat of Christ or the judgment seat of God. This judgment is not a judgment to determine whether we go to heaven or to hell. It is to determine the degree of reward or loss of reward to be given for faithfulness in Christian living. Paul told the believers in Rome, "So why do you condemn another believer? Why do you look down on another believer? Remember, we will all stand before the judgment seat of God" (Romans 14:10). No follower of Christ will escape this evaluation of his or her life.

The judgment seat was a familiar term in the Greek culture for a seat on which judgment was to take place by a ruler. Pilate sat on a judgment seat to give a hearing to Jesus' identity and his crimes (Matthew 27:19; John 19:13). The judgment seat was also the place from which a judge determined the winners in the Isthmian Games, the predecessor to the Greek Olympic Games. Paul used this athletic analogy to describe the effort we must make to be pleasing to the Lord and win the "prize" for "running well" (living faithfully). "All athletes are disciplined in their training. They do it to win a prize that will fade away, but we do it for an eternal prize. So I run with purpose in every step. I am not just shadowboxing. I discipline my body like an athlete, training it to do what it should. Otherwise, I fear that after preaching to others I myself might be disqualified [for the prize]" (1 Corinthians 9:25–27).

Another comparison Paul used to motivate Christians to live faithfully was the picture of a builder. The builder Paul speaks about is the one who is guiding, teaching, or leading other Christians.

Anyone who builds on that foundation [of a person's initial faith in Jesus Christ] may use a variety of materials—gold, silver, jewels, wood, hay, or straw. But on the judgment day, fire will reveal what kind of work each builder has done. The fire will show if a person's work has any value. If the work survives, that builder will receive a reward. But if the work is burned up, the builder will suffer great loss. The builder will be saved, but like someone barely escaping through a wall of flames.

1 Corinthians 3:12–15

The "fire" in these verses is not hell. This fire is an image of how the works in our life will be evaluated. The believer isn't burned, but the deeds he has done in life are either burned or purified by the fire of God's evaluation. Works that were done with pure motives, with sound teaching from the Bible, and with wise, godly advice will be greatly rewarded by our Savior. Those works done with impure motives and selfish ambition will not be worthy of any reward or praise from Christ.

Humans don't know all the facts and can't know with certainty the heart of another person. Paul warned us about making final evaluations of a person's Christian ministry. "So don't make judgments about anyone ahead of time—before the Lord returns. For he will bring our darkest secrets to light and will reveal our private motives. Then God will give to each one whatever praise is due" (1 Corinthians 4:5). Of course, if a Christian confesses his sins to the Lord, these "dark secrets" (sins) are treated with amazing grace and mercy at the judgment seat of Christ (1 John 1:9). Hidden sins that are unconfessed will be treated differently and receive no reward.

The primary reward for faithfulness is the privilege of ruling together with Christ. Even in eternity, God will organize his followers in ways that will require leaders and rulers. This is taught in a parable given by Jesus in Luke 19:11–27. A nobleman went away to be crowned king, receive a kingdom, and return. He gave ten pounds of silver (about four months' wages) to each of his ten servants and told them to invest it for when he returned. By the time the nobleman-now-king returned to organize his kingdom, one servant had gained ten times his original amount. The king announced, "You will be governor of ten cities as your reward" (Luke 19:17). Another gained five times his amount and was given five cities to govern. But to one of the servants who didn't invest his money, the ten pounds of silver was taken away. He was rebuked as foolish, and did not receive the privilege of governing even one city.

There are several rewards in Scripture called "crowns." The twenty-four elders in Revelation 4–5 were sitting on thrones and wearing victory crowns like the ones promised to the overcomers in Revelation 2–3. The apostle Paul even lists some Christian qualities for which there is a special crown of victory. He mentions the crown of life given for those who patiently endure trials (James 1:12). The crown of glory is given to those who are faithful leaders in churches and other ministries (1 Thessalonians 2:19 NIV) (some translations call it the "crown of rejoicing"). Others include a crown that will last forever (1 Corinthians 9:25 NIV), and a crown of righteousness (2 Timothy 4:8). In Revelation 4:10, the twenty-four elders cast their crowns before the heavenly throne in worship. This does not suggest that they give their rewards back to God. Instead, it shows that they recognize even their faithful service to Christ was only possible by his mercy and grace.

The Time of the Judgment Seat of Christ. The judgment seat of Christ will take place in heaven immediately after the rapture. This was also discussed briefly in chapter 5. The twenty-four elders pictured in Revelation 4–5 represent the church, the body of Christ. The twenty-four elders function as priests and kings. It is interesting that during the time of David the priests of the Old Testament were organized into twenty-four orders or divisions. In the vision of Revelation 4–5, the twenty-four elders have already received their crowns (rewards), and they are already robed in white garments. In Revelation 19:8, the bride (the universal church) "has been given the finest of pure white linen to wear. For the fine linen represents the good deeds of God's holy people." In Revelation, the judgment seat of Christ has already taken place as the tribulation begins.

The Principles of the Judgment. Some principles of the believer's judgment have already been mentioned. Here are a few more: First, the judgment seat of Christ will be an individual judgment. Some of us might wish that our judgment would be an evaluation of a group we belong to, such as our church, our Christian parents, or our Christian friends. Instead, we must all come individually before the Lord of the universe to be evaluated. "For we must all stand before Christ to be judged. We will each receive whatever we deserve for the good or evil we have done in this earthly body" (2 Corinthians 5:10). Another version translates this verse, "For we must all appear *and* be revealed as we are before the judgment seat of Christ" (AMP-CE, italics original).

There is no punishment for the believer at this judgment, or in eternity. For some Christians, there may be some embarrassment at how they have lived. The apostle John wrote in one of his letters, "And now, dear children, remain in fellowship with Christ so that when he returns, you will be full of courage and not shrink back from him in shame" (1 John 2:28).

Second, those who communicate biblical truth to others will be examined with more scrutiny because of their greater influence. James, the half brother of the Lord and the leader of the early Jerusalem church, warned, "Dear brothers and sisters, not many of you should become teachers in the church, for we who teach will be judged more strictly" (James 3:1).

Third, believers will be given great mercy and grace at their evaluation if they have also treated others with the same mercy and grace. James explained, "There will be no mercy for those who have not shown mercy to others. But if you have been merciful, God will be merciful when he judges you" (James 2:13).

The Great White Throne Judgment

The name of this judgment is derived from the description John gives in Revelation 20:11–15. After Satan is thrown into the lake of fire at the climax of the millennial kingdom, John saw in his vision a great white throne. God was sitting on this throne and the "earth and sky fled from his presence" (v. 11). This description is designed to portray the awesome and holy character of God. All of the dead who had never believed in the one true God of Israel (Old Testament) or in Jesus as God's Messiah (New Testament) came before the great white throne. Everyone—both those buried in graves on land or buried at sea—was brought before the throne of God.

A search was made to find the names of any of these dead people in the Book of Life, the book that lists all who had received eternal life by faith in Jesus. "And the books were opened, including the Book of Life. . . . And anyone whose name was not found recorded in the Book of Life was thrown into the lake of fire" (vv. 12, 15). Before these people are thrown into the lake of fire, God will determine the degree of their punishment. The works of the genuine believer will be evaluated at the judgment seat of Christ to determine the extent of reward. In a corresponding manner, the works of the unbeliever will be evaluated at the great white throne judgment to decide the degree of punishment.

Jesus taught that the punishment on the people of Sodom, the wicked Old Testament city, would be less severe than on the city of Capernaum. This was because Capernaum received more direct information about God through the personal ministry of Jesus. They are more directly responsible for these truths about God. Elsewhere Jesus explained, "When someone has been given much, much will be required in return" (Luke 12:48). Jesus told the people of Capernaum, "It will be *more tolerable* for the land of Sodom on the day of judgment than for you" (Matthew 11:24 HCSB). That's what the apostle John meant when he concluded the scene of the great white throne judgment. "And the dead were judged according to what they had done, as recorded in the books" (Revelation 20:12).

To emphasize that death will never again occur in those who have come to faith, Revelation states, "Then death and the grave were thrown into the lake of fire. This lake of fire is the second death" (Revelation 20:14). Other versions of the first part of this verse translate, "Then Death and Hades were thrown into the lake of fire" (ESV). *Hades* is a word that describes the temporary place of punishment for all unbelievers as they wait for their final judgment at the great white throne. Hades is the place to which the rich man was assigned in Jesus' teaching in Luke 16:19–31. In the story, the rich man who lived for selfish pleasure and completely ignored the sufferings of a poor man named Lazarus ended up "in Hades . . . in torment" (Luke 16:23 ESV). Other Bible versions translate Hades with the common term, *hell* (NET, CEV, KJV). Hades, the temporary place of punishment, is thrown into the final place of punishment, the lake of fire.

Jesus spoke of the lake of fire in the parable of the sheep and the goats (discussed in chapter 11). To the goats, Jesus said, "Depart from me, you cursed, into the eternal fire prepared for the devil and his angels" (Matthew 25:41 ESV). Jesus also used the word *hell* to describe the lake of fire. He warned about people who would be "thrown into hell, 'where the maggots never die and the fire never goes out'" (Mark 9:48). Whatever name we assign to it, the place is a severe punishment and according to Jesus is an "eternal" fire.

New Heaven and New Earth

While there are several passages in the Bible that describe something of what heaven is like, there are many mysteries to heaven as well. The apostle Paul taught us that while death is an absolute blessing, we still do not see all that heaven will involve. He reminded us, "We live by faith and not by sight. We are confident, and we would prefer to leave the body and to be at home with the Lord" (2 Corinthians 5:7–8 CEB). In his ascension, Jesus was taken up into heaven (Acts 1:9–11). At the present time, the Lord is resident in heaven. The book of Hebrews tells us, "We have a High Priest who sat down in the place of honor beside the throne of the majestic God in heaven" (Hebrews 8:1).

Although we don't know where this heaven is, it clearly involves the personal presence of God the Father and Christ the Son. To be "at home with the Lord" means we go to heaven when we die and live spiritually in his presence. This heaven is where all other dead believers now live, believers from both the Old and the New Testaments. They live in spirit form, as a soul without a body, waiting for their ultimate, resurrected body. Some teachers of the Bible believe that in heaven we will be given temporary or intermediate bodies until the time for our resurrection. At least, the Bible suggests that in this spirit form in heaven, we will still be able to speak, to wear clothing, etc. For example, John said, "I saw under the altar the souls of all who had been martyred" (Revelation 6:9)—these "souls" were visible. "They shouted to the Lord and said" (6:10)—they could speak. "Then a white robe was given to each of them" (6:11)—they could wear clothes. Each of these characteristics seems to imply something like a body.

Many people have the misconception that Christians exist in a soul or spirit form for all eternity. Some assume we will spend eternity floating around on fluffy clouds, singing hymns and playing harps. This distorts the truth. Those who have received the free gift of eternal life will actually live forever on a new earth. When God created the universe (Genesis 1), he repeated the phrase "and God saw that it was good" (or a similar one) seven times. The earth was created specifically as a place for people to live. God also specifically created and designed physical bodies for Adam and Eve, and for all people. That too was very good. When sin entered the universe, death came into existence and killed the body. Yet God didn't cancel his design for the human body. He will replace the old body with a new, resurrected (and ultimately physical) body.

In some similar way, God will "resurrect" the earth and the heavens, re-creating both. Revelation 21:1 describes this as "a new heaven and a new earth." This takes place after the millennium comes to an end. *New* in the phrase "new heavens and new earth" means something radically new. When I buy a new car, it may be much newer than my previous car, but it may still be three or four years old. The word *new* in "a new heaven and a new earth" means a brand-new model, like the new car bought off the showroom floor. Although God doesn't give us a lot of details, we can expect that the new heaven and new earth will be spectacular. Since the terms are "a new *heaven* and a new *earth*," we must expect some continuity, some likeness, to the old earth and heaven we now know.

Ultimately, God will destroy the old heaven and the old earth. The Lord made a promise in the days of Noah not to destroy the earth again by another worldwide flood. At the end of the millennium, God will destroy the earth by fire. According to Peter, "The heavens will pass away with a terrible noise, and the very elements themselves will disappear in fire. . . . On that day, he [the Lord] will set the heavens on fire, and the elements will melt away in the flames. But we are looking forward to the new heavens and new earth he has promised, a world filled with God's righteousness" (2 Peter 3:10, 12–13). Peter is following closely the teachings of Jesus. "Heaven and earth will disappear, but my words will never disappear" (Matthew 24:35).

The things that are absent from the new earth are part of what characterizes it as new. Here is a simple list:

1. No sea (Revelation 21:1). Some think the sea represents God's enemies, especially Satan. Or perhaps it represents the judgment of God as in the time of the flood (Genesis 6:17). The oceans were the by-product of the flood in Noah's day. "No sea" may symbolize that God will never again judge the earth, since sin will not exist (cf. Genesis 9:11). In any case, for people, the sea is far less useful and much more dangerous than land.

2. No death, grief, crying, or pain (21:4). No tears will exist either. Here is the compassionate, personal touch of Christ. "He will wipe away every tear from their eyes."

3. No sin, such as no "cowards, unbelievers, the corrupt, murderers, the immoral, those who practice witchcraft, idol worshipers, and all liars—their fate is in the fiery lake of burning sulfur. This is the second death" (Revelation 21:8). The cowards seem to be those in the tribulation who reject Christ and out of fear of persecution take the mark of the Antichrist.

4. No temple (Revelation 21:22). The temple represented God's presence with people. In the New Jerusalem on the new earth, "The Lord God Almighty and the Lamb are its temple." In other words, God and Jesus will be personally present with people.
5. No curse (Revelation 22:3) and no night (21:23–25; 22:5).
6. No hunger or thirst or scorching heat of the sun (Revelation 7:16).

One more important thing can be added to this list. There will be no more spiritual thirst in eternity, for our thirst for God will be completely satisfied. The Lord knew that many will read through the book of Revelation without faith in Christ. If so, they may be seeking for God by the end of their reading. They will need to hear this last appeal to come to faith. Twice in the last two chapters of this book—the last two chapters of the Bible—Jesus announced that eternal life was a free gift from the Savior. No cost was involved in the faith that brings eternal life. "To the thirsty I will give water without cost from the spring of the water of life" (Revelation 21:6 NIV). Then a second time John writes, "The Spirit and the bride say, 'Come!' And let the one who hears say, 'Come!' Let the one who is thirsty come; and let the one who wishes take the free gift of the water of life" (Revelation 22:17 NIV).

Ultimately, the thing most new about the new earth is not that we will live with God in heaven but that God will come down to live with us on earth. "I heard a loud shout from the throne, saying, 'Look, God's home is now among his people! He will live with them, and they will be his people. God himself will be with them'" (Revelation 21:3).

The New Jerusalem

The most detailed description of the New Jerusalem is appropriately recorded in the last two chapters of the Bible, and most directly in Revelation 21:10–27. Along with the creation of the new heaven and the new earth will be a New Jerusalem, the eternal home for all believers. It is in the New Jerusalem that God's people will live in the presence of God forever. In fact, the New Jerusalem will be the central feature and the capital city of the new heaven and the new earth. The specific term *New Jerusalem* is only found twice in the Bible (Revelation 3:12; 21:2). The people themselves will maintain their earthly identity as Jews or Gentiles, Old Testament saints or members of the universal church. Of course, people never become angels—a misconception that some hold to. Angels will also maintain their distinction from humans.

Here are some other truths about the New Jerusalem.

Prepared. Unlike the new heaven and new earth, which are yet to be created, the New Jerusalem is already under construction in heaven. Three times in Revelation, the apostle John referred to Jerusalem as coming down from God out of heaven and descending to the new earth. Two are the references to the *New* Jerusalem as mentioned previously; the third is where Jerusalem is mentioned coming down in Revelation 3:10. This may be the place that Jesus meant when he promised the eleven disciples, "There is more than enough room in my Father's home. . . . When everything is ready, I will come and get you, so that you will always be with me where I am" (John 14:2–3).

Paul also wrote about the New Jerusalem as if it already existed. He described an analogy using Hagar and Sarah. Hagar was the female servant of Abraham's wife, Sarah (Genesis 16:1). Abraham fathered a son, Ishmael, with Hagar. Sarah was the principal wife of Abraham and mother of Isaac. She was never a servant. Paul compared Hagar to the Mosaic law given at Mount Sinai and to the Jerusalem in his time. "But the other woman, Sarah, represents the heavenly Jerusalem. She is the free woman" (Galatians 4:26). *Heavenly* emphasizes the origin of the New Jerusalem before it comes down to earth, not the place where it will be for eternity. For Christians, the heavenly Jerusalem is free from the Mosaic law and sin. In eternity, there will be no need for any form of the Mosaic law to tell us what we must do and not do. We will all know what is right, and we will never sin or break God's holy standards. Paul called on Christians to live that way now.

Pure. In contrast to the Jerusalem of the past, the New Jerusalem is called the "holy city" three times in Revelation 21–22. Of course, cities have no moral qualities by themselves. "Holy city" implies that all the people in the New Jerusalem will be fully pleasing to the Lord. Jesus was speaking of both the millennium and the new heaven and new earth that follow when he taught his disciples to pray, "May your Kingdom come soon. May your will be done on earth, as it is in heaven" (Matthew 6:10). Since there will be no sin in the New Jerusalem or in the people who live there, the Lord's purposes will be carried out completely for all eternity.

Protected. The Lord wants to encourage all believers in Christ that there will never be anything that can enter the city to harm us. There is no need for any form of protection in the city, for all evildoers will be cast into the lake of fire. Nevertheless, this new city will be built with regular reminders of our security. First, the walls of the city have twelve gates, guarded by twelve angels (Revelation 21:12). Since the city is laid out as a square, there are three gates on each of the four sides (v. 13). The walls are 216 feet thick (v. 17). This means the width of the walls are about 70 percent of the length of an American football field, and 60–65 percent of the length of a regulation soccer field. Now, that's wide.

Then, too, the gates of the city "will never be closed at the end of day because there is no night there" (21:25). No thieves will sneak into the city, no enemy warriors will force their way in, and no vicious animals will attack the city's citizens through the open gates. "Nothing evil will be allowed to enter, nor anyone who practices shameful idolatry and dishonesty—but only those whose names are written in the Lamb's Book of Life" (v. 27).

Populated. The names of the twelve tribes of Israel are written on the gates (21:12), and the names of the twelve apostles are written on the twelve foundation stones of the city (v. 14). This reminds us that all Old Testament and New Testament believers will live together in the New Jerusalem forever. Concerning those who have access to the New Jerusalem, John said, "The kings of the world will enter the city in all their glory. . . . And all the nations will bring their glory and honor into the city" (Revelation 21:24, 26). Who are these "kings of the world" and who are "the nations"? No details are given to answer these questions.

One possible explanation is that those people who are true believers and have lived through the millennium will not be resurrected. Instead, they will enter into the eternal state in transformed, sinless physical bodies like those of Adam and Eve before the fall. God will not abandon his purpose for humanity as created in Adam and Eve. In the same way, he will not abandon his ultimate purposes for the earth, so these millennial believers will marry and have children. God loves children, and will not abandon his design of reproduction either. This is why Revelation 22:2 says, "The leaves of the tree [of life] are for healing the nations" (NIV). All problems with their physical bodies will be cared for.

Permanent. Hebrews 11 speaks of Abraham, Isaac, and Jacob, living in tents as aliens or nomads, even when they reached the land God promised them. They had no permanent home at the time. Abraham lived by faith and "was confidently looking forward to a city with eternal foundations, a city designed and built by God" (Hebrews 11:10). He was looking forward to the New Jerusalem. Later, the author of Hebrews applies this truth to us: "For here we have no lasting city, but we seek the city that is to come" (Hebrews 13:14 ESV).

Picturesque. The New Jerusalem will be absolutely astounding with beauty. Revelation 21:2 says that John saw "the holy city, the new Jerusalem, coming down from God out of heaven like a bride beautifully dressed for her husband." A little later, he saw that the city "shone with the glory of God and sparkled like a precious stone—like jasper as clear as crystal" (Revelation 21:11). The foundation stones of the city are inlaid with twelve precious stones that are all named in Revelation 21:19–20. Each of the twelve gates of the city were made from a single, gigantic pearl. Nearly every precious and semiprecious jewel is mentioned in the construction or adornment of the city. Just like precious jewels are valued for their rarity, beauty, and durability, the New Jerusalem will be matchless, unusually striking, and eternal. Perhaps the New Jerusalem is most well-known for its main street made of pure gold, as clear as glass (Revelation 21:21).

Just as gold reflects beauty and glory, so God's beauty and God's glory are similar in Scripture. Sunshine itself has astounding beauty. Imagine every day with sunshine. In the New Jerusalem, "the city has no need of sun or moon, for the glory of God illuminates the city, and the Lamb is its light" (v. 23).

Preserving. The New Jerusalem is also a garden city. John saw a river with life-giving water "clear as crystal, flowing from the throne of God and of the Lamb" (Revelation 22:1). Our eternal life is like a constant flow of pure water that sustains us forever. The river "flowed down the center of the main street. On each side of the river grew a tree of life, bearing twelve crops of fruit, with a fresh crop each month" (Revelation 22:1–2). Many translations describe the productivity of the tree in verse 2 as "twelve kinds of fruit" each month (ESV, NET, HCSB, NASB, etc.).

Think of the Tree of Life as compared to *the apple tree.* This is a collective term that includes many such trees with different kinds of apples. On each side of the river that flows down the main street of the city, there may be many Trees of Life. The Tree of Life in the New Jerusalem expresses God's restoration of his personal relationship with people who had been lost in the garden of Eden (Genesis 2:9).

Pleasant. Think of the New Jerusalem as the most joyful place ever. The Lord told Isaiah,

> Look! I am creating new heavens and a new earth, and no one will even think about the old ones anymore. Be glad; rejoice forever in my creation! And look! I will create Jerusalem as a place of happiness. Her people will be a source of joy.
>
> 65:17–18

No one in the New Jerusalem will ever be depressed, discouraged, or despondent.

In the book of Hebrews, the author explains that when we come to Christ in faith or when Christians come to the Lord Jesus in prayer, we "come to Mount Zion, to the city of the living God, the heavenly Jerusalem, and to countless thousands of angels in a joyful gathering" (Hebrews 12:22). Angels have emotions. This verse describes the angels as joyful in the New Jerusalem. Mount Zion is a frequent Old Testament name for the hill on which the Jerusalem temple was located. The New Jerusalem will be a new temple where people and God will be together.

Personal. Nothing else about the New Jerusalem is more crucial than that it will be where the personal presence of God and his Christ will take up residence. As the New Jerusalem comes down to rest on the new earth, God comes down to reside in the New Jerusalem forever. Heaven (God's residence, not the planets or space) and earth unite and become one. God no longer makes his residence far from his people but lives on the new earth forever with his people.

The shape of the New Jerusalem is said to be "a square, as wide as it was long. In fact, its length and width and height were each 1,400 miles" (Revelation 21:16). This cube shape of the New Jerusalem recalls the same shape of the inner sanctuary of the earthly Jerusalem temple (cf. 1 Kings 6:20). The Old Testament tabernacle and temple were the place that God would meet with people. At Jesus' resurrection, he "entered that greater, more perfect Tabernacle in heaven, which was not made by human hands and is not part of this created world" (Hebrews 9:11). At the creation of the new earth, Christ and God the Father will reside in the New Jerusalem as it comes down to the new earth. The implication is that the entire New Jerusalem itself is God's temple, God's presence, on the new earth. Therefore, John saw "no temple in the city, for the Lord God Almighty and the Lamb are its temple" (Revelation 21:22).

The temple and city of Jerusalem on the old earth were copies of an eternal and heavenly model. What the old Jerusalem failed to be the New Jerusalem will fulfill: the ultimate "temple" where God will be among his people forever. John wrote, "I heard a loud shout from the throne, saying, 'Look, God's home is now among his people! He will live with them, and they will be his people. God himself will be with them'" (Revelation 21:3).

A Personal Relationship with God

The temple in the Old Testament was where God met with people personally. God could not live among people or be close to people because our sin separated us from God. Once every year, the high priest in Israel went into the Most Holy Place, the isolated, inner sanctuary of the temple. He passed through a large curtain that separated the Holy Place from the Most Holy Place, or Holy of Holies. The ark of the covenant was kept in this most inner sanctuary. The ark was the sacred chest or box in which was placed the stone tablets engraved with the Ten Commandments. (A few other things were placed there as well.) The high priest would place the blood of an unblemished sacrificial animal on the gold-overlaid lid called the "mercy seat." The mercy seat formed the top of the ark of the covenant.

This sacrifice for the sins of people was only sufficient to provide forgiveness for a year. When Jesus died, was resurrected, and ascended to heaven, he entered the temple, or sanctuary, in heaven itself. The earthly tabernacle and temple were modeled after the heavenly temple. Jesus made a once-for-all sacrifice of his own blood and thereby accomplished an eternal forgiveness (Hebrews 9:12). At the moment of Jesus' death, the curtain in the Jerusalem temple was torn in two from top to bottom. The curtain that prevented everyone but the high priest once a year from entering the Most Holy Place was now gone. This physically portrayed how those who believe in Jesus as their Messiah for their eternal forgiveness can now come into the personal presence of God the Father and our Lord Jesus Christ.

This sacrifice of Jesus on the cross and his resurrection from the dead two thousand years ago can bring us eternal life through which we enter into the personal presence of God. But this relationship requires personal faith on our part. We must be convinced that Jesus is our only provision for living in the New Jerusalem forever and escaping the lake of fire.

God is absolutely righteous, so righteousness is absolutely required to have a personal relationship with God. What kind of righteousness is required? It's certainly not our own righteousness. We don't have any personal righteousness. Isaiah offered a word picture to describe our righteousness. "We are all infected and impure with sin. When we display our righteous deeds, they are nothing but filthy rags" (Isaiah 64:6). Our external religious devotion or our compassionate works done for others cannot bring us righteousness or eternal life. As the apostle Paul explained, "people are counted as righteous [before God], not because of their work, but because of their faith in God who forgives sinners" (Romans 4:5).

We are not righteous in ourselves, but we can be counted as righteous before God because of Jesus' sacrifice for us. We cannot achieve righteousness from within ourselves. The apostle Paul, in his former life as a devoted Pharisee, claimed a near-perfect religious life as a Jew: "As far as a person can be righteous by obeying the commands of the Law, I was without fault" (Philippians 3:6 TEV). The righteousness that is needed to gain eternal life and be in personal relationship with God must be a righteousness that is given to us by God. When Paul met Jesus in a vision on the road to Damascus (Acts 9), he exchanged his own righteousness for the righteousness that God gives to a person on the basis of faith in Jesus, God's Son. Paul wrote, "Because of Him I have suffered the loss of all things and consider them filth, so that I may gain Christ and be found in Him, not having a righteousness of my own from the law, but one that is through faith in Christ—the righteousness from God based on faith" (Philippians 3:8–9 HCSB).

Do you have the righteousness that comes from God on the basis of faith in Jesus Christ? You can. In fact, you can enter into a personal relationship with God and Christ at this very moment by believing in Jesus. He is the only one who can by faith give you God's righteousness. He died and was raised from the dead to give you the gift of eternal life and the right to live with him in a future, new earth.

Dr. John Hart (ThM, Dallas Theological Seminary; ThD, Grace Theological Seminary) is professor of Bible at Moody Bible Institute, the author of *50 Things You Need to Know About Heaven,* and the editor/contributor of *Evidence for the Rapture: A Biblical Case for Pretribulationism.* Dr. Hart lives in Indiana.

Answers to Your Questions About Heaven

We all want to know what happens after we die. Will we go to heaven? What will we do there? Will we see our loved ones?

It turns out the Bible is filled with answers to your most important questions, explaining what heaven looks like, who will be there, and how to get there in the first place. In this book you will find clear explanations of these passages, giving you an honest and beautiful picture of our eternal home. Find comfort and peace in the truth about heaven.

50 Things You Need to Know About Heaven by Dr. John Hart

☙ BETHANY HOUSE

Stay up-to-date on your favorite books and authors with our free e-newsletters. Sign up today at bethanyhouse.com.

Find us on Facebook. facebook.com/BHPnonfiction

Follow us on Twitter. @bethany_house